My LITTLE

Merry Christmas
Lots of Love

D1081461

cocktails

THE ESSENTIAL RECIPE HANDBOOK

Publisher's Note:
Raw or semi-cooked eggs should not be consumed by babies, toddlers, pregnant women,
the elderly or those suffering from reoccurring illness.

This is a **STAR FIRE** book
First published in 2007

Publisher and Creative Director: Nick Wells
Project Editor: Cat Emslie
Photographer: Paul Forrester
Home Economist: Maria Costantino
Art Director: Mike Spender
Layout Design: Andy Thornhill
Digital Design and Production: Chris Herbert
Picture Research: Toria Lyle
Editorial Assistant: Chelsea Edwards
Proofreader: Dawn Laker

07 09 11 10 08

1 3 5 7 9 10 8 6 4 2

This edition first published 2007 by
STAR FIRE
Crabtree Hall, Crabtree Lane
Fulham, London SW6 6TY
United Kingdom

www.star-fire.co.uk

Star Fire is part of the Foundry Creative Media Co. Ltd
© 2007 The Foundry Creative Media Co. Ltd

ISBN 978-1-84451-739-8

A CIP Record for this book is available from the British Library upon request

All rights reserved. No part of this publication may be reproduced, stored in a retrieval system,
or transmitted in any form or by any means, electronic, mechanical, photocopying, recording or otherwise,
without prior permission in writing of the publisher.

Every effort has been made to contact copyright holders. We apologize in advance for any omissions and
would be pleased to insert the appropriate acknowledgement in subsequent editions of this publication.

Printed in Dubai

cocktails

THE ESSENTIAL RECIPE HANDBOOK

Gina Steer

STAR FIRE

Contents

Introduction

Cocktails have enjoyed a revival over the last couple of decades with cocktail bars opening in all major cities, either as a separate establishment or within a hotel. This has resulted in the popularity of both the Classic Cocktail and its exotic counterparts. Each country uses their native ingredients to produce glorious specialities that reflect their culture. But what is a cocktail? It is a drink that can be incredibly simple, or made more complex by using two or more liqueurs or by blending spirits and mixers.

In towns and cities, cocktail bars normally open in the late afternoon to early evening, with many offering a happy hour – thus increasing their popularity enormously and introducing cocktails to a wider audience. With this boost in popularity it is no surprise that more and more people are serving cocktails to their friends and family. Being quick and easy to make and shake, cocktails are both delicious and impressive. They can be quickly dressed up with garnishes that will wow your guests.

This book aims to simplify cocktails with a straightforward approach to their creation. There are a host of stunning recipes, from the classics, such as Bucks Fizz, to the more exotic, such as Sea Breeze, plus many other delicious drinks. As well as this range of recipes there are also hints and tips on the right glasses to use, garnishes, sweeteners and some useful tricks of the trade; everything that would ever be required to shake, rattle and roll.

Equipment

There is not much equipment required for making cocktails; some are necessary, some just make life easier.

Corkscrew

There are many on the market and it really is a question of personal preference. I would recommend buying a cheap corkscrew with a spiral cone, as these tend to last forever.

Cocktail Shaker

Has two essential uses: combines the ingredients quickly and easily, as well as chilling the drink when shaken with ice.

Cobbler Shaker or Standard Cocktail Shaker

Normally made of three pieces: a metal (usually stainless steel) outside casing, a lid and a tight fitting

cap. There is usually a built-in strainer and the inside is often made of glass. Some have a tap on the side for cocktails that do not need straining.

Boston Shaker Similar to a Cobbler Shaker and looks like the shakers used by professional bar tenders. Has no strainer and consists of two parts.

Mixing Glass

Used for stirring drinks not shaking. Rolling a cocktail refers to rolling the cocktail from one mixing glass to another.

Spoons

Long or short handled spoons are ideal to use as stirrers.

Blender

These are useful for crushing ice. You will not need a large blender – simply one small enough to sit on or under the bar.

Ice Tongs

For handling ice cubes – again a case of personal preference.

Juice Extractor and Strainer

Again there are many on the market, from a simple lemon squeezer with a small sieve over a glass jug to a smoothie machine with an outlet tap.

Pitcher

There are two types of pitcher:

The Metal Cocktail Pitcher

More common before the 1930s, this pitcher had a spout and lid and looked like a coffee pot.

The Glass Martini Pitcher

Popular in the 1940s and 1950s, this pitcher is a tall glass jug with a glass stirrer.

Cloths

For polishing glasses before using.

Garnishes and Decoration

Cocktail Sticks Ideal for garnishes, both the normal short sticks or wooden kebab sticks cut down to about 10 cm/4 in threaded with fruits and balanced across the glass.

Knives A small sharp knife to use to cut fruit. A canella knife – to remove thicker strands of citrus peel and to make spirals for garnishing.

Zester Good for making long thin shreds of citrus peel for use as a garnish.

Other Garnishes From umbrellas and fancy stirrers with a motif or an amusing animal, to flowers or vegetables, the choice again is personal.

Straws Ideal for long drinks – bendy or straight.

Measures

Knowing what the different measures are is vital to be able to mix a successful cocktail. Obviously you will need a measuring cup or jug as well as the measure cap that is on top of the cocktail shaker.

25 ml = 0.9 fl oz = 1 measure
50 ml = 1.7 fl oz = 2 measures
75 ml = 2.6 fl oz = 3 measures
100 ml = 3.4 fl oz = 4 measures
70 cl (1 bottle gin) = 700ml = 23.7 fl oz
75 cl (1 bottle wine) = 750 ml = 25.4 fl oz

Types of Glasses

All glasses should be absolutely spotless and even if washed in a dishwasher it is always a good idea to polish the glasses before use. Before starting, check how many measures your glasses hold then keep each size together.

Classic Cocktail Glass

Triangle shape (or V–shaped) with a long stem. Holds about 14 cl/5 fl oz.

Double Cocktail

A short glass with a saucer cup on a short stem. Holds about 23 cl/8 fl oz.

Hurricane or Pina Colada

A bulbous shaped tall glass on a medium high stem. Holds 40 cl/ 14 fl oz.

Margarita Glass

A straight–sided glass with a small bowl at the top of a tall stem with a wide saucer at the top of the glass. This gives a wide rim, which is perfect for the salt effect for serving Margaritas. Usually holds about 20 cl/7 fl oz.

Coupe

A short glass on a stem, about 15 cm/6 inches high with a wide–necked bowl about 10 cm/4 inches wide.

Old-Fashioned

A stubby glass with a thick base, cut glass or clear. Holds about 23 cl/8 fl oz. It was the original glass for a cocktail and is now most often used for all shorts such as Gin and Tonic.

Highball

A tall tumbler, normally clear. Holds 28 cl/10 fl oz.

Collins

A tall clear tumbler. Holds 34 cl/12 fl oz.

Fluted Champagne

A tulip shaped glass on a tall stem. Holds 14 cl/5 fl oz.

Champagne Saucer

A saucer shaped glass on a medium high stem. Holds 14 cl/5 fl oz. Not so popular these days.

Wine

A wide variety available – red wine glasses are larger than white, with a large bowl (for the nose) on a tall stem. They can be either crystal or plain glass and normally hold about 20 cl/7 fl oz, but it varies.

Punch Glass

Punch glasses are generally sturdy enough to withstand hot liquids and often either have a handle or sit in a metal holder. As they are normally shaped like short tumblers is it easy to eat the fruit that is often put in punches.

Ingredients

Liqueurs

Liqueurs like crème de cacao, crème de menthe and curaçao come in a variety of colours, but there is no noticeable difference in taste. Whilst the recipes may specify the use of a certain colour it is not necessary to strictly adhere to this recommendation; feel free to experiment with different shades.

Coconut Cream

Look for cans or packets of creamed coconut that are sweetened – the unsweetened varieties are designed for culinary purposes and are not suitable for using in cocktails. If you cannot find the sweetened varieties make your own as follows: chill a block of coconut cream and grate coarsely; add an equal amount of caster sugar; add freshly boiled water, a teaspoon at a time; stir until the sugar and coconut are well blended. It should have the texture of single cream, and if it is too sweet use slightly less sugar next time. Use as soon as possible after blending – do not keep, as it will quickly turn rancid.

Salt and Sugar

Table Salt This is ideal for frosting the rim of cocktails, especially sours – simply place a small amount in a saucer as wide as the glass. Dip the glass in water or egg white, shake off the excess and place in the salt. Press down until well coated then allow to dry before using.

Caster Sugar Use as above in place of salt for drinks that are sweeter.

Sugar Syrup Many recipes call for some sweetness. This can be either clear honey or sugar syrup. I would recommend making the syrup in small amounts and using it freshly made. After a long period the syrup could start to crystallize. Make sugar syrup as follows: use 225 g/8 oz white granulated sugar and 150 ml/¼ pt water; place the sugar and water in a heavy-based saucepan and place over a gentle heat; heat gently, stirring occasionally until the sugar has completely dissolved; bring to the boil and boil steadily (to a temperature of 105°C/221°F) until a light syrup is formed; remove from the heat. Leave to cool, then pour into a screw-top sterilized bottle. When cold, screw down the lid. Use as required.

Eggs

Eggs are used in order to make a drink sparkling clear; they do not affect the taste of the drink so can be left out if preferred. Do make sure that the eggs used are as fresh as possible. A good test for this is to place a raw egg in its shell in a bowl of water; if it sinks to the bottom it is fresh, but if it floats to the surface it is stale.

Milk and Cream

Again, make sure the milk or cream is very fresh, of the best quality and use chilled.

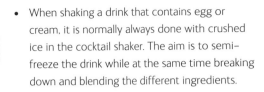

Fruit

Use fruits that are ripe and unblemished.

Ice

- The quality of the ice used in cocktails is of paramount importance. Water with a strong fluoride flavour or from a hard–water area will affect the taste of the drink. Ice is used in many cocktails to cleanse and give a crystal clear appearance. So use filtered or bottled still water, or use purification tablets to clean the water.
- Make ice on a regular basis; do not be tempted to make a large amount to keep in the freezer.
- Use crushed ice immediately as it will quickly dissolve.
- Crushed ice can be made in a blender, but you will need to check that your machine has metal rather than plastic blades. Before placing in the blender break the ice cubes down a little as follows (otherwise trying to crush them could seriously overload the blender motor): place the ice in a heavy–duty polythene bag and then in a clean tea towel; bash with a rolling pin or meat mallet, even a clean hammer will do; then place in the blender and whiz until crushed using the pulse button.
- In order to make broken ice simply follow the polythene bag stage for the making of crushed ice.
- When the recipe uses the crushed ice with the other ingredients in a cocktail shaker this is to produce a clear drink. Straining the cocktail from the shaker removes any unwanted particles (such as with citrus fruit juice) and any remaining crushed ice.

- When shaking a drink that contains egg or cream, it is normally always done with crushed ice in the cocktail shaker. The aim is to semi-freeze the drink while at the same time breaking down and blending the different ingredients.

Hints and Tips

There are a few guidelines that will significantly help make the mixing of cocktails easier:

- Keep all the ingredients to be used as cool as possible and, where applicable, such as with fruit juices, keep them in the refrigerator.
- Make sure that the work surface is clean and will not be ruined if some alcohol is spilled on it.
- Have a jug of warm water for rinsing purposes.
- When the weather is particularly hot, chill the glasses first.
- When serving warm or hot punches or cups, use heatproof glasses with stay–cool handles and warm the glasses before filling.
- Have to hand the prepared garnishes, straws, spoons and stirrers.
- Never try out a new cocktail on guests – try it yourself first, as it may need some adjustments.
- Do not waste malt whisky in a cocktail – these whiskies are designed to be drunk without mixers.
- Do not shake a drink that has a fizz in it.
- After shaking a cocktail that either has a very distinctive flavour or contains cream ALWAYS wash out the shaker before re-using.

Happy Shaking!

Aperitifs

As with many words we have adopted the word aperitif from the French – originally it was used to describe a liqueur drink that was taken before the meat in order to stimulate the appetite. Nowadays it is used to describe cocktails and the same drink can be referred to as either an aperitif or cocktail. Its purpose is not only to stimulate the appetite but as a relaxing prelude for what is to come. With this in mind, there are no hard and fast rules as to which flavoured drink should be served. It is all a matter of personal taste. So hence a cocktail is the perfect aperitif.

When deciding on which cocktail to serve, if your guests are staying for a meal, it would be a good idea to bear in mind the meal that will be served. If the meal is delicately flavoured and full of aromatic spices and ingredients, serving an aperitif that has a strong robust flavour will ruin the effect of the aromatic food. Whereas if the meal has a more robust flavour then a robust, strong–flavoured aperitif is fine.

It can be surprising when being served an aperitif as to the type of spirit or liqueur used. Brandy is always thought to be served only after a meal as a digestive but in fact makes a perfect cocktail such as in Brandy Sidecar or Brandy Classic.

This chapter has a host of classic cocktails, guaranteed to delight and enable you to serve the perfect cocktail before any meal. So get your cocktail shaker and get shaking!

Bloody Mary

Reputed to have been devised in Harry's Bar, New York, in 1921 it became all the rage in 1931 once prohibition had ended.

Ingredients SERVES 1

1 measure vodka

3 measures tomato juice

$^1\!/_2$ tsp lemon juice

2 dashes Worcestershire sauce

3–4 dashes Tabasco

pinch each of salt and freshly
    ground black pepper

celery stick as a stirrer

lemon slice to garnish

Method

Place all the ingredients except the celery and garnish into a cocktail shaker and shake for 1 minute. Strain into an old-fashioned glass (see page 9) and add the celery stick to use as a stirrer and garnish with a lemon slice.

Alternative

Place some ice cubes if liked in the glass before pouring the cocktail over. Replace the vodka with gin – this is known as Red Snapper.

Dry Martini

Perhaps the most famous cocktail of all thanks to Sean Connery when playing the suave, debonair James Bond. This was his choice of cocktail but he liked his 'shaken not stirred'. Here both methods are given.

Ingredients   SERVES 1

4 ice cubes
$^1/_2$ measure dry vermouth
3 measures gin
1 green olive or twist of lemon
    peel to garnish

Method 1

Place the ice cubes into a cocktail shaker and add the vermouth and gin. Stir with a long-handled bar spoon then strain into a chilled cocktail glass. Garnish with a green olive on a cocktail stick or twist of lemon peel.

Method 2

Place the ice, vermouth and gin in a cocktail shaker and shake vigorously for 1 minute. Pour into a frosted cocktail glass (see page 10) and garnish with an olive or lemon twist.

Alternative

To turn this drink into a Buckeye Martini simply garnish with a black olive instead of a green one.

Manhattan

This cocktail takes its name from New York's most popular lunch area, which boasts some of the trendiest lunch restaurants in the city.

Ingredients   SERVES 1

3–4 ice cubes, broken
2 measures rye whiskey or bourbon
1 measure sweet vermouth
4 drops Angostura Bitters
1 maraschino cherry on a stick

Method

Place the broken ice into a cocktail shaker. Pour in the rye whiskey or bourbon with the sweet vermouth and add the Angostura Bitters. Shake for 20 seconds then pour unstrained into a cocktail glass and garnish with the cherry.

Alternative

Replace the rye whiskey or bourbon with brandy to serve a Brandy Manhattan.

Screwdriver

There are a few theories as to the origins of the name of this famous cocktail. One is that a US oilman stationed in Iran was seen stirring his drink with his screwdriver, hence the name.

Ingredients   SERVES 1

4 ice cubes, crushed

2 measures vodka

4 measures freshly squeezed
   orange juice

1 small slice of orange and 1
   maraschino cherry to garnish

Method

Place all the ingredients except the garnish into a chilled cocktail glass and stir with a bar spoon. Garnish with the orange slice and cherry then serve.

Alternatives

The vodka can be replaced with either rum or gin and become a Screwdriver Rum or Screwdriver Gin.

Rusty Nail

The whisky liqueur Drambuie has overtones of honey and heather and is reputed to date back to Bonnie Prince Charlie.

Ingredients SERVES 1

2 ice cubes
1 measure Scotch whisky
$^1/_2$ measure Drambuie
lemon rind spiral to garnish

Method

Place the ice cubes into an old-fashioned glass (see page 9) and pour over the whisky. Place a bar spoon into the glass with the back of the spoon facing uppermost and pour over the Drambuie. Stir lightly with the bar spoon and serve garnished with the lemon rind spiral.

Frozen Daiquiri

Developed in Cuba around 1896 this very popular classic cocktail can be found on most bar menus. Try some of the other delicious variations that can be found.

Ingredients SERVES 1

4 ice cubes, crushed
freshly squeezed juice from
   2 ripe limes
1 tsp sugar syrup (see page 10)
2 measures white rum
lime wedge to garnish

Method

Place the crushed ice into a cocktail shaker and pour in the lime juice, sugar syrup and white rum. Shake for 1 minute or until the shaker feels very cold. Strain into the chilled glass. Serve garnished with the lime wedge.

Alternative

Try a Melon Daiquiri by adding 2 measures of Midori (Melon Liqueur) and only use 1 measure of freshly squeezed lime juice.

Whisky Mac

The popularity of this drink is such that many people do not realize that it is in fact a cocktail. It is a great winter warmer that is enjoyed across the world.

Ingredients   SERVES 1

2–3 ice cubes, broken
1 measure Scotch whisky
1 measure ginger wine

Method

Half fill an old–fashioned glass (see page 9) with the broken ice and pour over the whisky. Add the ginger wine, stir and serve.

Alternative

American dry ginger or ginger ale can be used in place of the ginger wine.

Brandy Sidecar

This was created in Paris just after the Second World War for an army officer who arrived at Harry's Bar in Paris in a sidecar and this was made especially for him.

Ingredients   SERVES 1

3 ice cubes
1 measure cognac
1 measure Cointreau
1 measure freshly squeezed
   lemon juice
lemon rind spiral to garnish

Method

Place the ice cubes into a cocktail shaker and pour over the cognac. Cointreau and lemon juice. Shake for 30 seconds then strain and pour into a chilled cocktail or old–fashioned glass (see page 9). Garnish with the lemon spiral and serve.

Alternative

1 teaspoon of sugar syrup can be added if liked.

Cosmopolitan

There are quite a few varieties of this cocktail; try these, then be adventurous and make up your own creation.

Ingredients   SERVES 1

4 ice cubes, crushed
1 measure gin
$^1/_2$ measure Southern Comfort
$^1/_2$ measure blackcurrant cordial
    or syrup
1 measure freshly squeezed lime juice
1 tsp egg white
lime slice to garnish

Method

Place the crushed ice into a tumbler. Pour all the other ingredients into a cocktail shaker and shake for 1 minute or until thoroughly blended. Strain into the ice–filled glass and serve garnished with a lime slice.

Alternative

Ingredients

4 ice cubes, crushed
1 measure vodka
1 measure Cointreau
1 measure cranberry juice
$^1/_2$ tsp lemon juice
orange twist to garnish

Method

Place all the ingredients except the ice into a cocktail shaker, shake for 20 seconds or until blended. Place the crushed ice into a short tumbler, pour the shaken cocktail over the crushed ice then serve garnished with a twist of orange.

New Yorker

This classic cocktail has a few variations all depending on the type of whisky used; for example, if using rye whiskey, add 1 teaspoon of grenadine and add $^1/_2$ teaspoon of sugar, then it is called a Red New York.

Ingredients   SERVES 1

2 measures Scotch whisky
$^1/_2$ measure freshly squeezed
    lime juice
1 tsp grenadine
4 ice cubes, crushed
orange slice to garnish

Method

Place all the ingredients except for the crushed ice into a cocktail shaker and shake for 1 minute. Place the crushed ice into a short tumbler. Pour over the cocktail, garnish with an orange slice and serve.

Napoleon

This cocktail contains Fernet Branca which is an aromatic bitter spirit made from over forty herbs and is mainly made these days in Milan.

Ingredients   SERVES 1

2–3 ice cubes, broken
2 measures gin
$1/2$ measure Dubonnet
2–3 dashes curaçao
dash Fernet Branca or
   Angostura Bitters

Method

Place all the ingredients into a cocktail shaker and shake for 1 minute or until blended. Strain into an old–fashioned glass (see page 9) over the broken ice and serve immediately.

Alternative

Try using Grand Marnier instead of curaçao, for a slightly sweeter taste.

Pink Gin

In 1824 a doctor who was treating the Venezuelan army for stomach ailments developed a remedy from local grown bitter herbs. This later became known as Angostura Bitters. It was the British navy who discovered a new use for the remedy by adding a few drops of gin, it gave the drink a whole new dimension.

Ingredients   SERVES 1

4 dashes Angostura Bitters
2 measures gin
    (Plymouth or London)
iced water

Method

Chill a glass until frosty. Pour in the Angostura Bitters and swirl the glass until the base is coated with the Bitters. Discard any remaining Bitters. Pour in the gin, stir, then serve with iced water and dilute to taste.

White Lady

This is a very popular classic cocktail that has a few varieties. Use either London or Plymouth gin although these days London gin is more usual.

Ingredients   SERVES 1

2 measures gin
1 measure Cointreau
1 tsp freshly squeezed lemon juice
$^1/_2$ tsp egg white
2 ice cubes, crushed (optional)
lemon rind spiral to garnish

Method

Place the gin, Cointreau, lemon juice and egg white into a cocktail shaker and shake for 30 seconds until blended. Strain into a cocktail glass filled with the crushed ice if using and serve garnished with the lemon spiral.

Alternatives

Substitute the Cointreau with grenadine for a Pink Lady and the lemon juice with grapefruit juice for a Fair Lady.

Old–Fashioned

It is commonly believed that President Roosevelt mixed this cocktail for King George VI and Queen Elizabeth and it apparently went down a 'storm'.

Ingredients SERVES 1

2 measures bourbon
few drops Angostura Bitters
few drops sugar syrup (see page 10)
orange slice and maraschino cherry
    to garnish

Method

Place the bourbon, Angostura Bitters and sugar syrup in a cocktail shaker and shake for 30 seconds until blended. Pour into a chilled old–fashioned glass (see page 9) and serve garnished with the orange slice and cherry on a stick.

Alternative

Fill the old–fashioned glass with crushed ice and pour the shaken cocktail over. Serve with a stirrer.

Collinson

As its name suggests, this cocktail is based on the same format as a Collins but it has an unusual twist with the addition of the kirsch. Orange bitters is a liqueur made from the peel of unripe or sour oranges steeped in gin or other alcohol.

Ingredients   SERVES 1

1 dash orange bitters
1 measure gin
$^1/_2$ measure dry vermouth
$^1/_2$–1 measure kirsch, according
   to taste
2 ice cubes, crushed
thinly pared lemon rind strip

Method

Place the orange bitters into a cocktail shaker with the gin and dry vermouth, and kirsch to taste. Shake for 30 seconds then pour into a Collins glass (see page 9) filled with the crushed ice. Add the lemon rind and serve with a stirrer.

Salty Dog

Give this cocktail a touch of sparkle by adding a Margarita twist to the drink and frost the edge of the glass with grapefruit juice and salt. Allow it to dry before using.

Ingredients   SERVES 1

2 measures gin
4 measures grapefruit juice
4–5 ice cubes, broken
1 lime slice to garnish

Method

Frost the glass (see page 10) Pour the gin and grapefruit juice into a cocktail shaker and shake for 30 seconds. Place the broken ice into a tumbler and strain in the gin and grapefruit. Garnish and serve immediately.

Alternative

To make a Greyhound serve in a plain glass. Replace the gin with vodka.

Between the Sheets

Often a cocktail is served chilled but without the ice being present in the serving glass. This is achieved by placing the ingredients and crushed ice into a cocktail shaker and then shaking until a frost forms on the outside. The cocktail is then strained into the glass.

Ingredients SERVES 1

4 ice cubes, crushed
1½ measures brandy
1 measure white rum
½ measure Cointreau
1 tsp freshly squeezed lemon juice
1 tsp sugar syrup (see page 10)
lemon butterfly twist to garnish

Method

Place the crushed ice with the brandy, white rum, Cointreau, lemon juice and sugar syrup in a cocktail shaker. Shake for 1 minute or until thoroughly chilled and a frost appears on the outside of the shaker. Strain into a cocktail glass, garnish and serve.

Alternative

Leave out the sugar syrup for a cocktail with more bite.

Beachcomber

A cool refreshing drink that is ideal on a long hot sunny day. Try serving at summer parties without much alcohol content as it is perfect for keeping the heat out without spoiling the party mood.

Ingredients   SERVES 1

3 ice cubes, crushed
1 measure green crème de menthe
100 ml/3^1/$_2$ fl oz soda water
    or lemonade
1 mint sprig to garnish

Method

Place the crushed ice into a tumbler and pour over the crème de menthe. Top up with the soda water or lemonade and stir. Garnish with a mint sprig and serve immediately.

Sea Breeze

Back in the 1930s this cocktail was made with gin, grenadine and lemon juice. However, over the years it has developed into this very popular, and has to be said, delicious cocktail.

Ingredients   SERVES 1

1 measure vodka

2–3 measures (or to taste)
cranberry juice

1–2 measures (or to taste)
grapefruit juice

4 ice cubes

orange slice and fresh cranberries if
available, to garnish

Method

Place the vodka in a cocktail shaker
and add the cranberry and grapefruit
juice to taste. Shake until blended.
Place the ice into a tumbler, pour
the cocktail over and serve
garnished with an orange slice
and a stirrer.

Alternative

Replace the grapefruit juice with
pineapple juice to make a
Bay Breeze.

Harvey Wallbanger

There are a few stories regarding the naming of this famous drink. One of them relates to Harvey, a Californian surfer who added Galliano to a Screwdriver – he loved it so much he ordered quite a few. On trying to leave he bounced and bumped his way out from one wall to the next until he found the door – hence the Harvey Wallbanger was born.

Ingredients   SERVES 1

6–8 ice cubes

$^1/_2$ measure Galliano

1$^1/_2$ measures vodka

5 measures freshly squeezed
     orange juice

2 small orange wedges to garnish

Method

Place some ice cubes into a collins glass (see page 9) and pour over the Galliano. Place the vodka, orange juice and remaining ice into a cocktail shaker and shake until frosty. Strain then pour over the Galliano, garnish and serve with a stirrer.

Alternative

If liked pour the chilled vodka and orange over crushed ice then carefully pour the Galliano on top so it floats on the surface.

Rum Planter Cocktail

When a recipe calls for a little freshly squeezed citrus fruit, simply cut a small or medium sized wedge of fruit and place in a hand–held squeezer or simply just squeeze using your fingers.

Ingredients   SERVES 1

4 ice cubes, crushed

1 measure dark rum

1 tsp freshly squeezed orange juice

1 tsp freshly squeezed lemon juice

2 dashes Angostura Bitters

1 tsp caster sugar

tropical fruits to garnish, such as
    pineapple, mango and banana

Method

Place the crushed ice into a cocktail shaker and add the rum with the orange and lemon juice, together with the Angostura Bitters and sugar. Shake for 1 minute or until a frost is formed on the outside of the shaker. Pour into a tumbler and garnish with small pieces of pineapple, mango and banana.

Alternative

Vary the fruits used for garnish. For a special occasion make a stunning garnish by threading small pieces of mango, kiwi, pineapple and papaya on to a short kebab stick and balance across the glass.

Sex on the Beach

If you are holding a party, and there are a few of the same cocktail required, double up the ingredients to speed up the waiting time, especially at the beginning of the party.

Ingredients   SERVES 1

$1/2$ measure vodka
$1/2$ measure peach schnapps
1 measure cranberry juice
1 measure freshly squeezed
    orange juice
3 ice cubes
1 slice peach to garnish (optional)

Method

Place all the ingredients into a cocktail shaker and shake for 30–45 seconds. Pour into a chilled tall glass and serve garnished with the peach slice and add a straw.

Alternative

For more variety, swap the peach garnish for a maraschino cherry and orange slice.

Adonis

Created in 1886 to celebrate the success of a Broadway show this cocktail quickly became popular both in the US and the UK. If you like a sweet drink, use sweet sherry, otherwise use the dry sherry, such as Tio Pepe, as used in the recipe.

Ingredients SERVES 1

2 measures dry sherry (Tio Pepe)
1 measure sweet rosso vermouth
1–2 dashes orange bitters or
orange curaçao
thinly pared orange rind spiral
to garnish

Method

Place all the ingredients except the orange rind into a cocktail shaker and blend for 20 seconds. Pour into a cocktail glass and serve garnished with the orange rind spiral.

Alternative

Use 1 dash of Angostura Bitters if liked in place of the orange bitters.

Tequila Sunrise

As the name suggests, this cocktail originated in Mexico around 1930. It was called Tequila Sunrise most probably due to the colours that are caught in the glass, which are similar to the beautiful sunrises found in Mexico.

Ingredients   SERVES 1

4 ice cubes
$^1/_2$ measure grenadine
2 measures tequila
120 ml/4 fl oz freshly squeezed
    orange juice
orange slice and maraschino cherry
    to garnish

Method

Place the crushed ice into a tall tumbler, then slowly pour the grenadine over the ice allowing it to sink to the bottom of the glass. Place the tequila and orange juice into a cocktail shaker and blend for 30 seconds. Strain into the glass and serve garnished with an orange slice, maraschino cherry and a straw.

Alternative

Try a Florida Sunrise, simply replace the orange juice with pineapple juice and garnish with a small wedge of pineapple.

Zombie

Created in 1933 in America's very first South Sea Island restaurant in order to complement the exotic food that was to be served there. It quickly became a great hit and other similar beach restaurants quickly sprang up.

Ingredients   SERVES 1

3 ice cubes

1 measure dark rum

1 measure white rum

$1/2$ measure apricot brandy

2 measures pineapple juice

2 measures freshly squeezed
    orange juice

1 measure lime juice

wedge of pineapple, maraschino
    cherry and mint sprig to garnish

Method

Place the ice into a cocktail shaker then pour in the other ingredients. Shake for 30 seconds then pour into a tall glass and serve garnished with a pineapple wedge, cherry and mint sprig. Serve immediately and add a straw to the glass.

Alternative

If liked frost the rim of the glass with lime juice and salt (see page 10).

Gin and It

This cocktail could be described as the original Martini and the first mention of a Martini was in 1862 with a drink called Martinez. This drink was made from sweet vermouth and gin. Gradually the sweet vermouth was replaced with dry vermouth and the Dry Martini was born. Gin and It was very popular in the 1940s and drunk mainly by women both during and after the Second World War.

Ingredients   SERVES 1
4 measures sweet rosso vermouth
1 measure gin
1 ice cube (optional)
1 maraschino cherry to garnish

Method
Place the sweet vermouth and gin into a cocktail shaker and shake for 30 seconds. Pour into a short tumbler, add the ice if using and garnish with the maraschino cherry on a cocktail stick.

Alternative
If liked, try shaking with broken ice before straining into the glass.

007 – Vodka Martini

This cocktail was made famous by the film star Sean Connery while playing James Bond when in the film he says these immortal words, 'Mine's a dry Martini, shaken not stirred'. Purists, however, would argue that a Martini should in fact be stirred not shaken. Whichever you choose – enjoy.

Ingredients   SERVES 1

3 measures vodka
1 measure dry vermouth (Noilly Prat)
twist of lemon
1 green olive to garnish

Method

Place the vodka into a cocktail shaker and pour in the dry vermouth. Shake for 20 seconds then pour into a cocktail glass and squeeze the lemon twist to release a few drops of juice then discard. Finally garnish with the green olive on a stick.

Alternative

Gin can be used in place of the vodka as can Bacardi rum.

Merry Widow

This cocktail is a mixture of cultures. One of the components of vermouth is the herb wormwood which, if taken in large quantities, can cause hallucinations. The sweet vermouth was developed in Italy in the eighteenth century while later in the nineteenth century the French developed the dry vermouth.

Ingredients   SERVES 1

2 measures gin

1 measure dry vermouth

1 teaspoon Benedictine

$^1/_2$ teaspoon Pernod

1 dash Angostura Bitters

Method

Place all the ingredients into a cocktail shaker and shake for 30 seconds. Strain into a cocktail glass and serve.

Bacardi Classic

It was in 1936 that a New York hotel bar and restaurant started serving this cocktail and without using Bacardi rum. After a visit by the makers of Bacardi rum, to the courts a temporary injunction was raised and later that year became permanent at the Supreme Court which stated that ONLY Bacardi rum should be used for this cocktail.

Ingredients   SERVES 1

1 ¹/₂ –2 measures Bacardi rum

1 measure lemon juice

1 tsp grenadine

1 tsp (or to taste, sugar syrup, see page 10)

2 ice cubes, crushed

1 maraschino cherry

Method

Place all the ingredients into a cocktail shaker and shake for 30 seconds. Pour into a cocktail glass and serve garnished with the cherry on a cocktail stick.

Alternative

Use the two measures of Bacardi rum if a stronger drink is preferred and replace the lemon juice with lime juice.

Gimlet

A gimlet is a small tool that is used to bore holes in wood and was often used to tap into barrels by inn keepers. Cocktails bearing the name Gimlet appeared around 1930 and it was used to describe a short sharp drink.

Ingredients   SERVES 1

2 measures gin
1 tbsp freshly squeezed lime juice
    or cordial
2 ice cubes, crushed
1 measure soda water
twist of lime to garnish

Method

Place the gin and lime juice into a cocktail shaker and blend for 20 seconds. Place the crushed ice into a short tumbler and strain over the ice. Add the soda water and serve with a lime twist and a stirrer.

Alternatives

Vodka, tequila and rum can all be used to replace the gin to suit any taste.

Brandy Classic

This cocktail gets its colour by the addition of blue curaçao. This attractive liqueur comes from the dried peel of the green orange that is grown in the Caribbean island of the same name.

Ingredients SERVES 1

1 measure brandy
1 measure blue curaçao
1 tbsp freshly squeezed lemon juice
1 tbsp syrup from a jar of
    maraschino cherries
3 ice cubes, crushed
lemon rind spiral and maraschino
    cherry to garnish

Method

Place the ingredients into a cocktail shaker and shake for 30 seconds. Pour into a cocktail glass and serve garnished with the lemon rind spiral and a maraschino cherry.

Alternatives

Try replacing the brandy with either gin or vodka or even white rum.

Luigi

Grenadine is made in France from pomegranates. It is a non–alcoholic drink, red in colour and is used to provide colour and sweetness with the delicate flavour of pomegranates.

Ingredients SERVES 1

1 measure freshly squeezed
    orange juice
1 measure dry vermouth
$^1/_2$ measure Cointreau
1 measure grenadine
2 measures gin
3 ice cubes
orange wedge to garnish

Method

Place all the ingredients into a cocktail shaker and shake for 30 seconds or until a frost forms on the outside of the shaker. Strain into a cocktail glass and serve garnished with an orange wedge and a stirrer.

French Leave

Pernod is made from the spice star anise that can be found in North Vietnam and Southern China. It is an aromatic spice used extensively in these areas to flavour many traditional dishes as well as drinks.

Ingredients   SERVES 1

2 ice cubes, crushed

2 measures vodka

1 measure Pernod

1 measure freshly squeezed
     orange juice

maraschino cherry, mint sprig and
     peach slice to garnish

Method

Place the ingredients into a cocktail shaker and blend for 30 seconds or until a frost forms on the outside of the shaker. Strain into a cocktail glass and serve, garnish with a maraschino cherry, mint sprig and peach slice.

Alternative

Replace the vodka with either brandy or gin.

Opera

In the Sixties, Dubonnet became a very popular drink especially with women but it now seems to have lost popularity as a drink on its own. However, it makes an excellent addition to any cocktail. A red wine based drink that is flavoured with an extract from the bark of a tropical tree, it was developed in France by Joseph Dubonnet around 1846.

Ingredients   SERVES 1

4 ice cubes
1 measure Dubonnet
$^{1}/_{2}$ measure yellow curaçao
2 measures gin
orange and lemon rind spirals
    to garnish

Method

Place two ice cubes into the cocktail shaker with the Dubonnet, curaçao and gin. Shake for 30 seconds. Place the remaining ice cubes into a cocktail glass, pour over the Dubonnet and gin and serve garnished with the orange and lemon rind spirals and a stirrer.

Alternative

Have fun by using one of the other varieties of curaçao – try blue, green or even red.

Stormy Weather

Sweet vermouth is an aromatic reddish brown wine–based drink originating from Italy and was developed in the eighteenth century. These days Martini Rosso and Cinzano are the most easily obtained sweet vermouths.

Ingredients
SERVES 1

2–3 ice cubes
2 measures gin
$^1/_2$ measure Mandarine
   Napoleon liqueur
$^1/_2$ measure dry vermouth
1 measure sweet rosso vermouth
   orange twist to garnish

Method

Place the ice cubes into a cocktail shaker with all the other ingredients. Shake for 30 seconds or until a frost forms on the outside of the cocktail shaker. Strain into a cocktail glass and serve garnished with an orange twist and a stirrer.

Black Widow

This cocktail has a definite kick to it and is not for the faint-hearted, combining the fruity flavours of peach and orange with a distinct hint of herbs and a good splash of Southern Comfort. Guaranteed to get any party going.

Ingredients
SERVES 1

3 ice cubes
2 measures dark rum
1–1$\frac{1}{2}$ measures Southern Comfort
freshly squeezed lime juice
1 tsp sugar syrup (see page 10)
lime slice

Method

Place the ice cubes into a cocktail shaker with all the other ingredients. Shake for 30 seconds then strain into a cocktail glass and serve garnished with the lime slice.

Alternative

Try a slice of lemon, rather than lime, as garnish.

Mad Dog

Crème de cacao is a chocolate liqueur and is normally made as a clear light liquid, but can be found as a dark, caramel colour. The delicious chocolate flavour is obtained from both the cocoa bean and the vanilla pod. The alcoholic content can vary and is often as high as 25%.

Ingredients
SERVES 1

3–4 ice cubes
1 measure tequila
1 measure crème de banane
1 measure dark crème de cacao
freshly squeezed juice from $^1/_2$ a lime
lime wedge and banana slice
  to garnish

Method

Place the ice cubes into a cocktail shaker and add the other ingredients. Shake for 30 seconds or until a frost forms on the outside of the shaker. Strain into a cocktail glass and serve garnished with the lime wedge and banana slice.

Alternative
Try white crème de cacao for a different effect.

Negroni

Campari comes from an infusion of bitter herbs, aromatic plants and fruits that are steeped in alcohol and water; it is classed with the 'bitters'. This cocktail originated from Italy around 1860 and its 60 ingredients are still a closely guarded secret even to this day.

Ingredients   SERVES 1

1 measure gin
1 measure sweet rosso vermouth
$^1/_2$ measure Campari
3 ice cubes, broken
1 measure soda water
orange twist to garnish

Method

Place the gin, sweet vermouth and Campari into a cocktail shaker and shake until blended. Three-quarters fill a short tumbler with broken ice and pour over the gin and vermouth mixture. Add the soda water, garnish and serve.

Crossbow

Decorating the rim of the glass is a fun thing to do and adds to the general mood of the party, showing your guests that you care. Try to vary the ingredients used, such as cocoa powder, sugar, salt or even ground spice.

Ingredients SERVES 1

1 tbsp finely grated chocolate

3 ice cubes

$^1/_2$ measure gin

$^1/_2$ measure dark crème de cacao

$^1/_2$ measure Cointreau

Method

Place the grated chocolate on a saucer and pour about 2 tablespoons of water in another. Dip a chilled cocktail glass in the water and then in the grated chocolate in order to coat the rim. Allow to set for about 5 minutes before using. Place the ice cubes into the cocktail shaker and pour in the gin, crème de cacao and Cointreau. Shake until well blended then pour into the chocolate rimmed glass and serve.

Skipper

There are many brands of Scotch whisky blends to choose from, so when using whisky for cocktails use whichever you prefer, but I would advise drinking the malts without accompaniment.

Ingredients   SERVES 1

3 ice cubes
$^1/_2$ measure grenadine
1 measure dry vermouth
3–4 measures Scotch whisky
freshly squeezed juice from
$^1/_2$ orange, preferably organic
orange twist to garnish

Method

Place the ice cubes into a cocktail shaker and add the grenadine, dry vermouth, whisky and orange juice. Shake for about 30 seconds then pour into a short tumbler and serve garnished with the orange twist.

Alternative

Look out for Skipper's Ripper – a rather different drink containing cola, granadine, rum and Southern Comfort.

Sours and Juleps

Sours first appeared on the party scene in the eighteenth century and the very first was the Brandy Sour. It is the cocktail that is ubiquitous to all Sours and from which many other flavoured sours have become popular. The standard Sours are as they sound, sour, mainly through the use of a substantial amount of freshly squeezed lemon juice and normally garnished with a piece of lemon either as a lemon rind spiral, or a lemon twist or wedge. Sugar or syrup can be added, but a minimal amount and often soda water is an optional extra. Any spirit can be used, from brandy, gin, vodka, rum or whisky. Liqueurs can also be used from Amaretto to Cointreau.

Created in the Southern States of America, juleps are the perfect answer to long hot sunny days and evenings. It is thought that the first juleps appeared in the eighteenth century and traditionally are made from just four ingredients but nowadays there are many variations on the original drink. As with food there are now no hard and set rules so feel free to experiment, but a word of caution: if you do, try at home first before offering to your friends or family.

Brandy Sour

It is widely believed that the first Brandy Sour to be mixed was around 1850 and was the beginning of a whole new drink experience. As the name implies, they contain very little sweetness and a large amount of lemon juice or similar sour flavouring.

Ingredients SERVES 1

3–4 ice cubes
2–3 dashes Angostura Bitters
3 tbsp freshly squeezed juice
   from 1 lemon
3 measures brandy
1 tsp sugar syrup (see page 10)
lemon twist to garnish

Method

Put the ice cubes into a cocktail shaker and sprinkle in the Angostura Bitters. Add the lemon juice, brandy and sugar syrup and shake for 1 minute or until a frost is formed on the outside of the shaker. Strain into a tumbler and serve garnished with a lemon twist.

Alternative
Replace the brandy with whisky.

Vodka Sour

For a change serve a sour as a long drink. Make as usual and then pour over 4–6 ice cubes placed in a highball glass (see page 9). Top up with soda water and serve with a stirrer.

Ingredients   SERVES 1

6 ice cubes
2 measures vodka
$^1/_2$ measure sugar syrup (see page 10)
1 egg white, preferably organic
2 measures freshly squeezed
    lemon juice
3 drops Angostura Bitters (optional)
soda water
lemon rind spiral to garnish

Method

Place two ice cubes into a cocktail shaker and add the vodka, sugar syrup and egg white. Shake briefly before adding the lemon juice and shaking for 30 seconds or until a frost is formed on the outside of the shaker. Place the remaining ice cubes into a highball glass, strain over the vodka mixture, top the glass up with soda water and serve garnished with the lemon rind spiral and a stirrer.

Alternative

This method would work with all Sours if liked.

Amaretto Sour

Amaretto is a sweet liqueur made from a basic infusion of almonds or of the kernels from the drupe fruit. It has a very distinctive almond or marzipan aroma and flavour. There are a few brands available, but the most well-known is Amaretto Disaronno.

Ingredients
SERVES 1

2 ice cubes
1$\frac{1}{2}$ measures amaretto liqueur
1$\frac{1}{2}$ measures freshly squeezed
   lemon juice
1 tsp sugar syrup (see page 10)
lemon twist to garnish

Method

Place the ice into the cocktail shaker and add the amaretto, lemon juice and sugar syrup. Shake for 30 seconds or until a frost forms on the outside. Strain into a small tumbler and serve garnished with a lemon twist.

Alternative

Ready-prepared sweet-and-sour mixes are an easy alternative to lime juice and sugar syrup.

Egg Sour

With this recipe it is important that the egg is very, very fresh. Do make sure that you prepare this cocktail as it is required, do not leave it standing around. Shake and serve, that is the trick with this cocktail.

Ingredients   SERVES 1

1 measure brandy

1 measure dry orange curaçao

1½ measures freshly squeezed
   lemon juice

1 very fresh small egg, lightly
   whisked

2 ice cubes, crushed

lemon slice to garnish

Method

Place the brandy into a cocktail shaker with the orange curaçao, lemon juice, lightly whisked egg and crushed ice. Shake for 20 seconds then strain into a short tumbler and serve garnished with a lemon slice.

Alternative

Add fine sugar to the shaker to sweeten to taste.

Bourbon Triple Sour

Triple sec is an almost colourless, orange flavoured liqueur developed by Jean–Baptiste Combier around 1834 in Saumur, one of the towns situated on the banks of the Loire River in France. It is used in many drinks mainly as a sweetener and also adds a hint of orange flavour.

Ingredients   SERVES 1

1 measure bourbon

1 measure triple sec

1$\frac{1}{2}$ measures freshly squeezed
    lemon juice

1 tsp sugar syrup (see page 10)

3 ice cubes, broken

lime slice and maraschino cherry to
    garnish

Method

Pour the bourbon, triple sec, lemon juice and sugar syrup into a cocktail shaker and blend for 20 seconds. Fill a tumbler with the broken ice, then strain the cocktail into the glass and serve garnished with the lime slice plus the maraschino cherry and add a stirrer.

Southern Tango

Many of the cocktails demand crushed ice. It is important that the water used to make the ice is of good drinking quality, otherwise as the ice melts into the cocktail it could affect the taste of the drink.

Ingredients SERVES 1

4 ice cubes
1 measure dry vermouth
1 measure Southern Comfort
2 measures lemonade

Method

When ready to serve, fill the cocktail shaker with the ice cubes and pour in the dry vermouth with the Southern Comfort. Shake for 30 seconds, then strain into the ice filled tumbler. Top up with the lemonade and serve immediately with a stirrer.

Alternative

To make this a true Sour pour the dry vermouth with the Southern Comfort and 2 measures freshly strained lemon juice and 1 teaspoon (or to taste) sugar syrup into a cocktail shaker. Shake all the ingredients together and serve in a short tumbler.

Caipirinha

Caipirinha is the national cocktail of Brazil and is normally made with the country's favourite brandy, cachaça, which is made from sugar cane. The name means 'peasant's drink'. It is made directly in the glass, never in a cocktail shaker.

Ingredients   SERVES 1

1 lime

1¹⁄₂–2 tsp caster sugar

4 ice cubes, broken

2 measures cachaça

Method

Cut the lime into small wedges and place with the sugar into an old-fashioned glass (see page 9). Using a spoon crush the lime wedges and sugar together until the juice flows out of the lime. Add sufficient broken ice to fill the glass then top up with the cachaça and serve.

Alternative

Many varieties of this cocktail are served the length and breadth of Brazil. These are often served with a variety of fruits in place of the lime. Try passion fruits, kiwi, pineapple, summer berries or grapes. Sometimes soy or dairy milk is added giving a creamy cocktail. Another alternative can be made by using vodka.

Scotch Melon Sour

Midori with its bright green colour is a melon–flavoured liqueur, and is an excellent addition to any drink. Being extremely sweet it is often added to drinks such as Sours to help modify the bitter tang. Vary the amount used to suit individual taste.

Ingredients
SERVES 1

4 ice cubes
1 measure Scotch whisky
1 measure Midori
2 measures freshly squeezed
    lemon juice
1 tsp sugar syrup (see page 10)

Method

Put the ice cubes into an old–fashioned glass (see page 9). Pour the remaining ingredients into a cocktail shaker and shake for 30 seconds then strain into the ice–filled glass and serve with a stirrer.

Alternative
Use other fruit–based liqueurs in place of the Midori; try kirsch, Cointreau or framboise.

63

Pisco Sour

Pisco is a brandy that is made by distilling Muscat wine. It has been an integral part of Peruvian culture for many years and even if no wine is consumed during a meal it is inconceivable not to have a glass of pisco after the meal.

Ingredients   SERVES 1

3 ice cubes, crushed
$1/2$–1 measure freshly squeezed
    lime juice
2 measures pisco
1 tsp sugar syrup (see page 10)
2 tsp egg white, preferably organic,
    lightly whisked
1 dash Angostura Bitters
wedge of lime to garnish

Method

Place the crushed ice into a tumbler then squeeze the lime juice over the crushed ice. Pour the remaining ingredients into a cocktail shaker and shake for 30 seconds. Pour over the ice and serve garnished with a wedge of lime.

Rob Roy

This cocktail is named after the Scottish hero Rob Roy who lived in the seventeenth century and has been described by many as the Scottish Robin Hood.

Ingredients   SERVES 1

1–2 ice cubes, broken
1 measure Scotch whisky
1 measure sweet vermouth
2 dashes Angostura Bitters
lemon rind spiral and maraschino
    cherry to garnish

Method

Place the broken ice into a cocktail glass then pour the remaining ingredients into a cocktail shaker and shake for 30 seconds. Pour over the ice and serve garnished with the lemon rind spiral and maraschino cherry.

Alternative

For a Dry Rob Roy, use dry, rather than sweet, vermouth. Or for a Perfect Rob Roy use equal parts sweet and dry vermouth.

Scorpio

When serving cocktails, presentation is very important: take care when cutting fruit twists to discard any pips and keep the slice thin but still intact. It is a good idea to cut some garnishes earlier then cover lightly and keep in the refrigerator.

Ingredients   SERVES 1

5 ice cubes, crushed

1 measure brandy

$^1/_2$ measure white rum

$^1/_2$ measure dark rum

2 measures freshly squeezed
  orange juice

$^1/_2$ measure Amaretto Disaronno

2–3 dashes Angostura Bitters

Method

Place half the ice into a cocktail shaker and add the brandy, white and dark rum with the orange juice, Amaretto Disaronno and Angostura Bitters. Shake for 1 minute or until a frost is formed on the outside of the shaker. Strain into a glass, add the remaining crushed ice and serve with a stirrer.

Alternative

Use all dark or white rum if preferred.

Mojito

One of the most popular summer cocktails around today. This Cuban drink has become the 'wow' both in London and New York regardless of the weather. There are many variations and part of the fun is experimenting with the ingredients to discover which ones best suit your taste buds.

Ingredients   SERVES 1

4 ice cubes, crushed
2–3 mint sprigs
2 measures white rum
3 tbsp freshly squeezed lime juice
2 tsp (or to taste) demerara sugar
soda water
fresh mint sprig to garnish

Method

Place half the crushed ice into a glass and add the mint sprigs. Carefully crush the mint on the ice. Pour the rum, lime juice, sugar and remaining ice into a cocktail shaker and shake until a frost forms on the outside. Pour into the glass, top up with soda water and garnish with a fresh mint sprig, and serve with a stirrer.

Alternative

Try using other flavoured rums such as dark rum or even fruit–flavoured rums, such as mango flavoured.

Clover Club

Many cocktails first appeared around the time of the lifting of Prohibition in the United States and this cocktail is just one of these. It first appeared around 1925 in one of the most popular bars in New York.

Ingredients SERVES 1

3 ice cubes

1¹/₂ measures gin

1 measure freshly squeezed
   lemon juice

1–2 tsp (or to taste) grenadine

1 small egg white, preferably
   organic, lightly whisked

Method

Place the ice into a cocktail shaker and add the remaining ingredients. Shake for 30 seconds then strain into a cocktail glass. Garnish with a twist of lemon rind and serve.

Alternative

Add 3 sprigs of mint to a glass half filled with crushed ice and lightly crush the mint on the ice. Mix the cocktail as above then pour over the mint–flavoured crushed ice. This then becomes a Clover Leaf.

Vodka Sazerac

The Vodka Sazerac is reputed to be the first ever cocktail and was developed by a Creole immigrant, Antoine Peychaud, who also created Peychaud Bitters. The cocktail was later adopted by the Cubans.

Ingredients   SERVES 1

3 ice cubes, broken
1 sugar cube
2 drops Angostura Bitters
3 drops Pernod
2 measures vodka
lemonade to serve

Method

Place the sugar cube into an old–fashioned glass (see page 9) and add the Angostura Bitters and Pernod. Using a stirrer, push the sugar cube around the glass. Add the vodka then top up with the lemonade and serve.

Alternative

Try experimenting and use different flavoured vodkas; choose a fruit flavour such as orange, lemon, peach or even a herb, but bear in mind the aniseed flavour of the Pernod.

Mint Julep

The word 'julep' is thought to have come from an ancient Arabic word meaning 'rose water'. It was not until the eighteenth century that the first mention of julep occurred in the United States and it quickly caught on, so that by the nineteenth century it had been thoroughly Americanized.

Ingredients   SERVES 1

4 ice cubes, crushed

4 fresh mint sprigs

1 measure sugar syrup (see page 10)

3 measures bourbon

2–3 fresh mint sprigs to garnish

Method

Place the mint sprigs into a tumbler and add the sugar syrup. With the back of a bar spoon gently crush the mint and sugar syrup to extract the mint flavour. Remove the crushed sprigs. Slowly stir in the bourbon then add the crushed ice. Place the fresh mint with the stalks down and the leaves facing upwards into the glass. Serve with a straw.

Alternative

Some Mint Juleps are served without crushing the mint and sugar syrup together. Simply fill a tumbler with crushed ice and pour over the sugar syrup then slowly stir in the bourbon. Add the mint sprigs and serve.

Southern Mint Julep

The Southern Mint Julep is as its name implies, synonymous with the Southern States of America. Traditionally juleps were served in silver or pewter cups and held by the drinker only at the base and top edge of the cup. This allowed a frost to form on the outside of the cup, and was meant to portray gentility.

Ingredients   SERVES 1

4 ice cubes, crushed

4 fresh mint sprigs

1 measure sugar syrup (see page 10)

1 measure Kentucky bourbon

3 measures Southern Comfort

Method

Place the mint sprigs into a tumbler and add the sugar syrup. Slowly stir in the bourbon and Southern Comfort then add the crushed ice. Place the fresh mint with the stalks down and the leaves facing upwards into the glass; serve with a straw and stirrer.

Champagne Julep

In the United States, juleps were originally made with brandy rather than bourbon and with this recipe, brandy is the ideal spirit to use with champagne.

Ingredients   SERVES 1

1–2 ice cubes, crushed

1 measure sugar syrup (see page 10)

2 measures brandy

3 measures champagne

2–3 fresh mint sprigs to garnish

Method

Place the crushed ice into a champagne flute and pour over the sugar syrup and then the brandy. Gently pour in the champagne and add the mint sprigs, with the leaves facing uppermost. Stir gently with a stirrer and serve.

Alternative

Though brandy is best, bourbon can be used instead.

Jungle Juice

Pisang Ambon is a very sweet, bright green liqueur from Indonesia and is made from herbs and green bananas. It works well when blended with orange juice or orange flavoured liqueur such as Cointreau.

Ingredients   SERVES 1

4 ice cubes, crushed
2 whole ice cubes
1 measure Pisang Ambon
$1/_2$ measure brandy
1 measure gin
4 measures freshly squeezed
   orange juice
2 tsp freshly squeezed lemon juice
3 mint sprigs

Method

Place all the ingredients into a cocktail shaker except for the crushed ice. Shake for 1 minute or until a frost forms on the outside of the cocktail shaker. Strain into a tumbler then add the ice cubes, the mint sprigs with the leaves pointing up, and serve.

Alternative

Add 1 measure of Cointreau to the above cocktail and top the glass up with soda water.

73

Jungle Wild

When using fresh mint or any herb to garnish a drink it is important to ensure that the herb is clean and free from any insects. Check carefully and if necessary rinse lightly, gently brushing off any dirt with your fingers, then allow it to dry on kitchen paper before using.

Ingredients   SERVES 1

4 ice cubes, crushed

1 measure white rum

1 measure Wild Turkey bourbon

$^1/_2$ measure Pisang Ambon

2 measures papaya juice

2 tbsp freshly squeezed juice
   from 1 lime

2 measures lemonade

3 sprigs fresh mint

Method

Place the crushed ice into a tumbler and pour over the white rum and Wild Turkey bourbon with the Pisang Ambon. Stir with a bar spoon then add the papaya juice and the strained lime juice. Top up with the lemonade and garnish with the mint sprigs.

Alternative

Thread the papaya wedges on to a cocktail stick and place across the top of the glass.

Knockout

The joy of this drink is the surprise of the cool delicious mint flavour of this white cocktail. If you cannot find white crème de menthe use the green variety; the flavour will be the same, just the surprise and colour will be different.

Ingredients   SERVES 1

4 ice cubes, crushed
2–3 mint sprigs
1 measure dry vermouth
1 measure white crème de menthe
2 measures gin
1 dash Pernod
lime slice to garnish

Method

Place the crushed ice into a tumbler and add the mint sprigs, dry vermouth and crème de menthe. Stir gently with a bar spoon then slowly stir in the gin and Pernod. Stir again then garnish with the lime slice and serve.

Champagne and Sparkles

Champagne is the wine of celebration and its mere mention can bring a smile of pleasure and anticipation to all. It is said that it can make the young wise and the old young. It is served at weddings, special occasions, has launched a thousand ships and shared many romantic occasions between two people. It should be served with style and the rules that apply to champagne also apply to champagne cocktails.

The wine should be served at the correct temperature in long-stemmed flute or tulip shaped glasses that will enhance the flow of bubbles to the crown of the glass and to concentrate the aroma. More bubbles will form on a crystal glass than on a plain glass. This is due to the rougher surface texture of the crystal glass. Champagne should be served at around 7°C and if chilled in the refrigerator, taken out a little while before opening as the refrigerator temperature should be kept at 5°C. To chill a bottle from room temperature, half fill a champagne bucket with ice and leave the bottle in for 30 minutes.

Take care when opening a bottle of champagne: only remove enough of the gold foil as to twist the wire hood, keeping a finger or thumb on the cork in case it 'pops'. Carefully ease the cork out, turning the bottle not the cork. So when serving champagne cocktails, it is worth bearing these points in mind so as to serve the perfect cocktail.

Kir Royale

Champagne cocktails were originally served as an aperitif before a formal dinner; however, they became so popular that it was not long before they were served at any time, day or night.

Ingredients   SERVES 1

$^1/_2$ measure crème de cassis

4 measures freshly opened
    chilled champagne

Method

Pour the crème de cassis into a champagne flute and top up with the freshly opened champagne. Stir lightly then serve immediately.

Alternative

A Kir Royale is often served with a whole strawberry in the glass. After adding the crème de cassis, simply add the lightly rinsed strawberry then top up with the champagne. Stir lightly and serve. This is an ideal drink for a romantic occasion or for Valentine's Day.

Classic Champagne Cocktail

The origin of this cocktail remains a mystery but is thought to have been created around 1850 in the American South. In 1888 a cocktail competition was organized by a US journalist and the winner was a John Doherty who produced this recipe, which he claimed came from a Southern US State.

Ingredients SERVES 1

2 dashes Angostura Bitters

1 sugar cube

3 measures chilled freshly
    opened champagne

$^1/_2$ measure cognac

orange twist to garnish

Method

Place the sugar cube into a champagne flute and shake the Angostura Bitters bottle over the sugar cube. Pour in the champagne and cognac, stir lightly then serve garnished with an orange twist. Serve immediately.

Alternative

If liked add a squeeze of lemon or orange before adding the champagne and cognac. Use the same fruit that has been squeezed into the cocktail as a garnish.

Great Idea

The word 'champagne' is a generic term that is used to describe a high quality sparkling white wine, produced in the Champagne area of France. Normally produced by small growers who then sell their grapes to the champagne houses of France, only wine that has been made from grapes grown in this area can be called champagne.

Ingredients   SERVES 1

1 measure pineapple juice
1 measure mandarin juice
$^{1}/_{2}$ measure maple syrup
3 measures chilled freshly
    opened champagne
1 small wedge of pineapple
    to garnish

Method

Pour the pineapple and mandarin juice into a champagne flute and add the maple syrup. Stir with a swizzle stick until the syrup has dissolved in the juice. Carefully pour in the chilled champagne and serve garnished with a small wedge of pineapple.

Alternative

If liked, cava (a sparkling wine from Spain) method champagne (a French sparkling wine that is not from the Champagne region) or New World sparkling wines can be used instead of champagne.

Bucks Fizz

There are quite a few recipes for different flavoured 'Bucks', none of which is as well known as this classic recipe. The term 'Buck' refers to the fact that the ingredients have been poured directly into a chilled tall glass and does not necessarily contain champagne.

Ingredients   SERVES 1

2 measures freshly squeezed
    orange juice
4 measures chilled and freshly
    opened champagne
orange twist to garnish

Method

Pour the orange juice into a champagne flute and top up with the chilled champagne. Stir lightly with a swizzle stick then serve immediately, garnished with an orange twist.

Black Velvet

This cocktail was created in London around the time that Prince Albert died – 1861. The story is that a royal steward decided that as the whole country was in mourning so should champagne be, so he created this cocktail which became very popular with both royal and commoner alike.

Ingredients   SERVES 1

4 measures Guinness
4 measures chilled freshly
    opened champagne

Method

Pour the Guinness into a champagne flute and top up with the chilled champagne. Serve immediately.

Alternative

Replace the Guinness with lager, using equal quantities of lager and champagne. This is then a Halsted Street Velvet.

Black Russian

Kahlúa is a coffee liqueur made from the finest Mexican coffee beans, cane spirit and a hint of vanilla. It also contains vodka and is sweetened with cane sugar. It was not imported to the States until the Sixties, but is now one of the most popular liqueurs.

Ingredients   SERVES 1

4 ice cubes, crushed
1¹/₂ measures vodka
1 measure Kahlúa
4 measures chilled cola
lemon spiral

Method

Place the ice cubes into a tall chilled tumbler, add the Kahlúa then slowly stir in the chilled cola. Serve immediately, garnished with a lemon spiral.

Alternative

Use a chocolate stick as a swizzle stick for added sweetness and flavour.

Bellini

When making a champagne cocktail it is important that the champagne has been chilled and opened just before drinking for maximum pleasure. When storing champagne it is best to store the bottle horizontally so as the wine is kept in contact with the cork – this prevents the cork from drying out.

Ingredients   SERVES 1

2 measures vodka
$1/_2$ measure peach schnapps
1 tsp peach juice
chilled freshly opened champagne
    to top up
peach slice to garnish

Method

Pour the vodka, peach schnapps and peach juice into a cocktail shaker and shake for 20 seconds. Pour into a chilled champagne flute then top up with the chilled champagne. Serve immediately, garnished with the peach slice.

Alternative

Use puréed peach instead of schnapps and peach juice, for a slightly thicker, less alcoholic drink.

New Orleans

When beginning to make cocktails perhaps one of the most important things to remember is to measure accurately and not to add more than is stated. If you do you may find that not only does the drink become unpalatable due to an overriding taste it could have the effect of making your guest drunk rather quickly – thus ending a party quicker than anticipated.

Ingredients   SERVES 1

3 ice cubes
1 measure white rum
$^1/_2$ measure peach brandy
1 tsp freshly squeezed orange juice
freshly opened chilled champagne
    to top up

Method

Place the ice into a cocktail shaker and add the rum, peach brandy and orange juice. Shake for 30 seconds then pour into a champagne flute, top up with champagne and serve.

Disaronno Mimosa

When choosing the champagne to use in a cocktail, choose carefully. Do not be tempted just because it is going to be mixed with a spirit, liqueur or fruit juice to buy the cheapest possible; this will certainly affect the taste but on the other hand, do not use the most expensive, as that is just a waste. Choose a middle–of–the–road bottle and make sure that it is well chilled and opened when required.

Ingredients   SERVES 1

$^1/_2$ measure Amaretto Disaronno
2 measures freshly squeezed orange
    juice, strained
2 measures freshly opened
    chilled champagne
orange twist to garnish

Method

Pour the Amaretto Disaronno and then the strained orange juice into a champagne flute. Stir then top up with the champagne and garnish with the orange twist.
Serve immediately.

Cherry Champagne

Maraschino cherries were originally produced for royalty and the wealthy and were considered a great delicacy. The cherries are preserved in brine, drained and steeped in alcohol and finally sweetened in a syrup that has the addition of food colouring. The red maraschino cherries are flavoured with almond while the green coloured cherries are flavoured with peppermint.

Ingredients   SERVES 1

2 ice cubes, crushed
$^1/_2$ measure cherry brandy
4 measures freshly opened
   chilled champagne
3–4 maraschino cherries to garnish

Method

Place the ice cubes into a champagne flute and pour over the cherry brandy. Top up with the chilled champagne and serve garnished with the cherries threaded on to a cocktail stick and placed across the rim of the glass.

Alternative

Try replacing the cherry brandy with 1 measure of kirsch and add 2 teaspoons of the syrup from the jar of maraschino cherries. Instead of fresh cherries, float a maraschino cherry in the cocktail.

Champagne Charlie

This cocktail is named after the founder and owner of the very famous champagne house, Heidsieck, which started producing champagne in 1851. His skills as a salesman and his good-time image earned him the name 'Champagne Charlie'.

Ingredients   SERVES 1

2–3 ice cubes, crushed

1 measure apricot brandy

4 measures freshly opened
  chilled champagne

1 rose petal or orange twist
  to garnish

Method

Place the crushed ice into a champagne flute and pour in the apricot brandy. Top up with the chilled champagne and serve garnished with the rose petal floating on top, or an orange twist.

Champagne Napoleon

It is said that on the eve of battle in 1814, Napoleon was explaining his battle plans to Monsieur Moët and it is reputed he said, 'In case I fail, I wish to reward you for the way you have conducted your business' – and with that he took off from his uniform jacket the Chevalier Cross of the Legion of Honour, which he promptly gave to Monsieur Moët.

Ingredients   SERVES 1

2 ice cubes
$^1/_2$ measure Mandarine Napoleon
1 measure freshly squeezed and
     strained orange juice
4 measures freshly opened
     chilled champagne
orange twist and 1
     maraschino cherry

Method

Place the ice cubes into a cocktail shaker and add the Mandarine Napoleon and the strained orange juice. Shake for 20 seconds then pour into a champagne flute and top up with champagne. Garnish with an orange twist and a cherry.

Alternative

Briefly stir the ingredients, rather than shaking, before topping up with the champagne.

Horn of Plenty

Grand Marnier is similar to Triple Sec as it is a blend of cognac, distilled essence of orange and other undisclosed ingredients and was created in 1880 by Alexandre Marnier–Lapostolle. It has a 40% alcohol content.

Ingredients   SERVES 1

2 ice cubes, crushed

1 measure Grand Marnier

$^1/_2$ measure Campari

$^1/_2$ measure grenadine

3 measures freshly opened
   chilled champagne

Method

Place the crushed ice into a champagne flute and pour in the Grand Marnier, Campari and grenadine. Stir to mix then top up with the chilled champagne and serve.

Alternative

Cava or sparkling wine can be used in place of the champagne if liked.

Henry's Special

Once champagne or any sparkling drink such as cava or sparkling wine has been opened it quickly loses its fizz. If you do not use all the bottle try this way of keeping the fizz in. Place a teaspoon, bowl end uppermost, in the open bottle. Store in the refrigerator. This will keep the bubbles in the wine for up to 24 hours.

Ingredients   SERVES 1

2 ice cubes
$^1/_2$ measure brandy
1 measure freshly squeezed
   grapefruit juice
1 tsp freshly squeezed lemon juice
1 level tsp clear honey
3 measures freshly opened
   chilled champagne
long cinnamon stick to use as stirrer

Method

Place the ice into a cocktail shaker and add the brandy, grapefruit, lemon juice and clear honey. Shake for 20–30 seconds or until well blended. Strain into a champagne flute and top up with the chilled champagne. Serve with the cinnamon stick to use as a stirrer.

Alternative

If liked, gently warm the honey before adding to the shaker, and place the crushed ice directly into the chilled champagne flute. This will make the drink slightly sweeter. Use a honey drizzler if liked to drizzle the honey into the shaker.

Night and Day

Campari is an alcoholic aperitif that is an infusion of bitter herbs with aromatic plants and fruits, which are then steeped in alcohol. The red colour comes from cochineal. It is classified as a 'bitter'. As with many of the liqueurs it originated in Italy and the original secret recipe is still used to this day.

Ingredients   SERVES 1

1 measure cognac
$^{1}/_{2}$ measure Grand Marnier
$^{1}/_{2}$ measure Campari
2 ice cubes, crushed
3 measures freshly opened
    chilled champagne
fresh strawberry to garnish

Method

Pour the cognac with the Grand Marnier and Campari into a cocktail shaker and shake for 30 seconds or until blended. Place the crushed ice into a champagne flute and pour over the cognac mixture. Top up with the chilled champagne and serve garnished with the strawberry.

Alternative

Replace the cognac with a fruit flavoured brandy.

Snowball

This used to be very popular with the ladies in all the trendy drinking spots throughout the UK and Europe during the Sixties and fitted in perfectly with the mood of the times. Nowadays it is still popular in Northern Europe. It is a delicious low alcoholic drink, perfect for those who do not want to miss out, but are watching their alcohol intake.

Ingredients   SERVES 1

3 ice cubes

2 measures advocaat

$^1/_2$ measure freshly squeezed and
    strained lime juice (or use
    lime cordial)

5 measures lemonade

2 maraschino cherries threaded on
    to a cocktail stick to garnish

Method

Place the ice into a tumbler and pour over the advocaat and then the lime cordial. Stir, then top up with the lemonade and serve garnished with the cherries.

Alternative

Replace the lemonade with chilled cava or sparkling wine to give the drink a bit of a kick.

Gagarin

Named after the USSR's first cosmonaut, this cocktail features vodka, another staple icon of Soviet culture. When serving vodka many purists state that the spirit should be kept cold at all times and with that in mind vodka is often kept in the freezer.

Ingredients   SERVES 1

2 ice cubes
1 measure vodka
$^1/_2$ measure cherry brandy
$^1/_2$ measure crème de cassis
1 tsp freshly squeezed lemon juice
3 measures dry Babycham
maraschino cherry

Method

Place the ice cubes together with the vodka, cherry brandy, crème de cassis and lemon juice into a cocktail shaker. Shake for 30 seconds or until a frost forms on the outside. Pour into a champagne flute, top up with the Babycham and serve garnished with the maraschino cherry.

Alternative

Use champagne or cava in place of the Babycham.

New Orleans Dandy

Rum is a spirit made from the by–products of sugar cane. The most well known rum is dark rum, but there are various others such as white rum, which is light–bodied and has a subtle flavour and is usually used as a mixer; Golden Rum is more full–bodied with a smooth mellow taste. There is also Spiced Rum, which can be white, golden or dark in colour and is infused with fruit spices. Try and enjoy.

Ingredients SERVES 1

3 ice cubes
1 measure white rum
$^1/_2$ measure peach brandy
1 tsp freshly squeezed orange juice
1 tsp freshly squeezed lime juice
4–5 measures freshly opened
    chilled champagne
orange and lime slice to garnish.

Method

Place the ice cubes into a cocktail shaker and pour in the rum together with the peach brandy, the orange and lime juice. Shake for 20 seconds then strain into a champagne glass. Top up with the champagne and serve garnished with an orange and lime slice.

White Witch

Beware of this cocktail – it may look innocent enough being almost pure white in colour but in fact its looks belie its effect – it has a hefty kick even though the taste is pure magic.

Ingredients   SERVES 1

4 ice cubes
1–2 measures white rum
$^1/_2$ measure white crème de cacao
$^1/_2$ measure Cointreau
1 tbsp lime juice
soda water to top up
lime slice to garnish

Method

Place half the ice cubes into the cocktail shaker with the white rum, crème de cacao and Cointreau. Add the lime juice then shake for 30 seconds. Place the remaining ice cubes in an old-fashioned glass (see page 9) then strain the cocktail into the glass. Top up with soda water and serve garnished with a lime slice.

Bouncing Bomb

No one is really sure where the name for this cocktail came from. Many believe it was created during the Second World War by the US airmen when on leave and relaxing.

Ingredients   SERVES 1

4 ice cubes
2 measures brandy
1 measure curaçao
soda water to top up
orange twist to garnish

Method

Place the ice cubes into a cocktail shaker and add the brandy and curaçao. Shake for 30 seconds. Pour into a highball glass (see page 9) and top up with soda water. Serve and decorate with an orange twist.

Alternative

You can vary the spirit used, so try bourbon, vodka or gin.

Horse's Neck

This cocktail gets its name from the traditional garnish which is a long lemon rind spiral that is used to decorate the glass.

Ingredients   SERVES 1

3 ice cubes
$1\frac{1}{2}$ measures brandy
ginger ale to top up
long lemon rind spiral to garnish

Method

Place the ice into a glass and pour in the brandy. Top up with the ginger ale then hang the lemon rind spiral on the glass rim and serve.

Alternative

The brandy can be replaced with other spirits if preferred. Try gin, vodka or whisky.

Gin Sling

It is widely believed that 'Slings' were first created in America and the name comes from a German word meaning 'to swallow quickly', the idea being that 'you sling the drink down your neck as quickly as possible'. Originally a Sling was only made using still cold water, but nowadays a sparkling water is more normal.

Ingredients
SERVES 1

4 ice cubes

2 measures gin

$^1/_2$ measure sugar syrup (see page 10)

1 measure freshly squeezed
lemon juice

2 measures chilled water, sparkling
or still, according to taste

pinch of freshly grated nutmeg

lemon twist to garnish

Method

Place the ice into a tall glass and pour over the gin, sugar syrup and lemon juice. Stir then top up with the chilled still or sparkling water and serve sprinkled with the freshly grated nutmeg and garnished with the lemon twist.

Alternative

Replace the gin with the same amount of brandy, vodka, rum or bourbon.

John Collins

A Collins is an ideal drink for the hot weather. Normally it is not shaken but made and served in a tall glass with a spirit such as bourbon, plus lemon or lime juice, sugar syrup (see page 10) and topped up with soda water.

Ingredients SERVES 1

4 ice cubes, crushed
2 measures bourbon
1 measure freshly squeezed
   lemon juice
$^1/_2$ measure sugar syrup
chilled soda water to top up
lemon slice to garnish

Method

Place the ice cubes in a chilled tall glass such as a highball glass (see page 9) then pour over the bourbon, the lemon juice and sugar syrup. Stir with a swizzle stick then top up with soda water, garnish with a lemon slice and serve.

Alternative

There are many variations to a John Collins. Try a Rum Collins by replacing the bourbon with rum – or a Mint Collins – here replace the bourbon with vodka and add a measure of crème de menthe.

Tom Collins

Originally this would have been made with 'Old Tom Gin', a gin sold in London when Prohibition was in force. A certain Captain Dudley Bradstreet hung up a sign in the shape of a cat and called it 'Old Tom'. The customers would put an amount of money in its mouth and from its paw (via a tube) a measure of gin would flow.

Ingredients   SERVES 1

3 ice cubes

2 measures gin

1 measure freshly squeezed
    lemon juice

$^1/_2$ measure sugar syrup (see page 10)

5 measures soda water

lemon or lime twist to garnish

Method

Place the ice into a tall chilled highball glass (see page 9) and pour in the bourbon, freshly squeezed lemon juice and sugar syrup. Stir lightly then top up with the soda water and serve garnished with the lemon or lime twist.

Alternative

Other 'Collins' drinks include a Sandy Collins, with Scotch whisky, or a Brandy Collins.

Singapore Sling

There are two ways of making a Sling: either make the cocktail then pour into an ice-filled glass or all the ingredients can be shaken together in a cocktail shaker, except for the soda water then strained into a glass.

Ingredients   SERVES 1

3 ice cubes, crushed
1 measure gin
1 measure cherry brandy
$^1/_2$ measure Benedictine
$^1/_2$ measure freshly squeezed
   lime juice
4 measures freshly squeezed
   orange juice
soda water to top up
small wedge pineapple and a fresh
   cherry to garnish

Method

Pour the gin, cherry brandy and Benedictine into a cocktail shaker. Strain in the lime and orange juice and shake for 30 seconds or until blended. Place the ice cubes into a collins glass (see page 9) and pour over the cocktail. Top up with soda water, add a swizzle stick and garnish with the pineapple wedge and cherry.

Alternative

A Raffles Singapore Sling is not topped up with soda water and is a short drink unlike the Singapore Sling.

Apricot Cooler

Coolers are prepared in the same manner as a Collins and served in the same kind of glass. They often contain a long spiral or twist of citrus rind and contain any kind of spirit. Normally they are not shaken unless containing egg white.

Ingredients   SERVES 1

4 ice cubes
2 measures apricot brandy
1 measure freshly squeezed
   lemon juice
1 tsp grenadine
2–3 dashes of Angostura Bitters
2 measures soda water
2 measures lemonade
lemon rind spiral to garnish

Method

Place the ice cubes into a collins glass (see page 9) and pour in the apricot brandy, lemon juice, grenadine and Angostura Bitters. Stir lightly then top up with the soda water and lemonade. Serve garnished with the lemon rind spiral and add a swizzle stick.

Moscow Mule

This cocktail was created by an American spirit distributor, John Martin. Before 1930 vodka was unknown in the US and after John Martin had bought the rights he started to market the sale of vodka. Whether by chance or design, he met up with two friends, one who had a glut of ginger beer – hence the Moscow Mule was created.

Ingredients SERVES 1

3 ice cubes, crushed
2 measures chilled vodka
freshly squeezed juice from 2 limes
ginger beer to top up
slice of lime to garnish

Method

Place the crushed ice into a chilled tall glass such as a highball (see page 9) and pour over the vodka then the freshly squeezed strained lime juice. Stir with a swizzle stick or bar spoon, top up with ginger beer and serve garnished with a lime slice.

Alternative

Try using different flavoured vodkas – try cherry, lemon, coconut, chocolate or even a herb flavoured vodka. Whichever you choose, remember to keep it chilled.

Vodka Twist Fizz

A Fizz is similar to a Collins but is always shaken before the fizz is added. It normally does not contain very much ice so as not to inhibit the fizz of the drink. Normally served in the morning or at midday with a swizzle stick and a straw.

Ingredients   SERVES 1

2 ice cubes

2 tbsp freshly squeezed lime juice

$^1/_2$ tsp sugar syrup (see page 10)

1 medium egg white,
    preferably organic

3 dashes Pernod

3 measures vodka

ginger ale to top up

lime slice to garnish

Method

Place the ice cubes into a cocktail shaker and strain in the lemon juice. Add the sugar syrup with the egg white, Pernod and vodka. Shake for 45 seconds or until well blended and a frost starts to form on the outside of the shaker. Pour into a chilled highball glass (see page 9) half-filled with ice and serve topped up with ginger ale and garnished with the lime slice; add a straw and a swizzle stick.

Alternative

If liked replace the Pernod and ginger ale with grenadine and soda water and add the freshly squeezed juice from 1 small orange.

Cuba Libre

It is widely believed this cocktail was created by American soldiers celebrating the end of the Spanish–American War and Cuba's freedom.

Ingredients SERVES 1

3 ice cubes, crushed
1 tbsp freshly squeezed, strained lime juice
2 measures Bacardi rum
5 measures cola
orange spiral to garnish

Method

Cut the squeezed lime shell in half and place in a chilled highball glass (see page 9). Pour the lime juice into the glass. Spoon in the ice then pour over the rum and top up with the cola. Add a straw and a swizzle stick and garnish with an orange spiral.

French '75

The very first 'French' was created in Paris during the First World War and this cocktail takes its name from the French '75 light field gun that was used during the war. French '75s are made in tall glasses such as a collins (see page 9).

Ingredients   SERVES 1

1 measure gin
1 measure freshly squeezed
   lemon juice
1 tsp caster sugar
4 ice cubes
5 measures freshly opened
   chilled champagne
1 maraschino cherry to garnish

Method

Pour the gin and lemon juice into a chilled collins glass and sprinkle in the sugar. Stir until the sugar has dissolved then add the ice cubes. Pour in the champagne and serve with a straw and a maraschino cherry.

Alternative

Replace the gin with either bourbon or cognac.

Long, Short and Creamy Cocktails

This chapter encompasses a large range of cocktails, which include long cocktails served in tall glasses designed not only to provide a taste of alcohol but also to quench the thirst on long hot sunny days or warm balmy evenings. Some have the addition of cream giving a smooth luxurious feel to the cocktail and helping to promote a feeling of well-being and happiness. Most of them contain more than five fluid measures of liquid before shaking.

Other cocktails in this chapter are short, less than five measures before shaking and are normally served in short glasses rather than a cocktail glass. These cocktails have a little more of an impact and are not designed to be sipped slowly, however neither are they meant to be drunk in a 'down in one' action.

When using cream in a cocktail it is advisable to use the freshest possible and to keep it in the refrigerator. Double cream is the best to use as its creaminess and thickness means that it will not separate out once it is poured into the glass. When coconut cream is called for, again do use as fresh as possible. Once a carton or can is opened, pour into a glass jug or bowl, cover with cling film or tin foil and store in the refrigerator. Use as quickly as possible and please do not be tempted to use in a drink after 2 days of opening.

Brandy Alexander

The Brandy Alexander is the original cocktail around which all the other Alexanders are based. It became popular in the early twentieth century. Allegedly the name originates from Alexander the Great who apparently wept as there were no more worlds for him to conquer.

Ingredients   SERVES 1

3 ice cubes
1 measure brandy
1 measure dark crème de cacao
1 measure double cream
grated nutmeg to garnish
chocolate stick or a swizzle stick
    to serve

Method

Place the ice into a cocktail shaker and pour in the brandy, crème de cacao and cream. Shake for 30 seconds or until thoroughly blended then pour into a short glass. Sprinkle the top with a little freshly grated nutmeg and serve with a chocolate stick or a swizzle stick to stir.

Alternative

Replace the grated nutmeg with a little grated plain dark chocolate. The brandy can be replaced with white or dark rum, or Amaretto liqueur.

Frostbite

You get a much better flavour and aroma from nutmeg if it is freshly grated. It is possible to buy small graters that are specifically designed for grating nutmeg. However if you do not possess one, a normal grater works just as well.

Ingredients   SERVES 1

3 ice cubes
1 measure tequila
1 measure double cream
1 measure white crème de cacao
freshly grated nutmeg to garnish

Method

Place the ice cubes into a cocktail shaker and add the tequila, double cream and white crème de cacao. Shake for 30 seconds or until well blended then strain into a short tumbler and serve sprinkled with a little freshly grated nutmeg.

Alternative

Add ½ measure of blue curaçao to achieve a more frostbitten effect!

White Russian

Tia Maria is a coffee liqueur made using Jamaican Blue Mountain coffee beans which are blended with cane spirit, sugar and vanilla, and allowed to ferment until an alcohol is produced. It can be drunk over ice, by itself or as part of a cocktail.

Ingredients   SERVES 1

4 ice cubes
1 measure vodka
1 measure Tia Maria
1 measure double cream
little freshly grated chocolate
    to garnish

Method

Place two ice cubes into a cocktail shaker and add the vodka, Tia Maria and the double cream. Shake for 30 seconds or until well blended. Place the two remaining ice cubes into a short tumbler and strain over the cocktail. Sprinkle the top with the grated chocolate and serve with a straw if liked.

Alternative

If preferred the double cream can be replaced with full fat milk for a slightly less creamy cocktail.

Angel's Treat

There is no hard and fast rule whether you use milk or dark chocolate in this cocktail. It is a question of personal taste; the only thing to remember is that when using chocolate, as with all ingredients, it is always worth using the best you can afford.

Ingredients SERVES 1

1 ice cube

1¹/₂ measures dark rum

1 measure Amaretto liqueur

2 tbsp whipped cream

2 tsp finely grated chocolate

Method

Place the ice into a cocktail shaker and add the rum, the Amaretto liqueur and 1 tablespoon of the whipped cream. Add 1 teaspoon of the grated chocolate then shake for 30 seconds or until blended. Strain into a short tumbler and float the remaining whipped cream on top. Sprinkle with the remaining grated chocolate and serve.

Alexander's Sister

Another cocktail that is based on the Brandy Alexander. This one has a distinct coffee aroma and flavour. Try frosting the rim of the glass using one tablespoon of grated chocolate and water. Simply dip the glass in the water, then the chocolate, and allow it to dry. Sprinkle the cocktail with a little grated chocolate if liked.

Ingredients

SERVES 1

4 ice cubes
1 measure dark rum
1 measure Kahlúa
1 measure double cream
freshly grated nutmeg or chocolate

Method

Place the ice cubes into a cocktail shaker and add the rum, Kahlúa and double cream. Shake for 30 seconds or until well blended then strain into a cocktail glass and serve garnished with the freshly grated nutmeg.

Alternative

There are many variations with Alexanders and one very easy one is to use one measure each of brandy, cream and Kahlúa. Simply shake until blended then strain into a cocktail glass and serve.

Margarita

The story is that the Margarita was created in the late 1940s for the well-known actress, Marjorie King, as she was allergic to all spirits except for tequila. There are many variations on the classic recipe, all of which are delicious.

Ingredients   SERVES 1

1 measure freshly squeezed
   lemon juice
1 tbsp salt
2 measures tequila
1$^1/_2$ measures triple sec
$^1/_2$ measure blue curaçao
$^1/_2$ measure freshly squeezed
   lemon juice

Method

Frost the glass (see page 10) and allow to dry. Place the tequila in a cocktail shaker with the triple sec, blue curaçao and $^1/_2$ measure of lemon juice. Shake for 30 seconds until blended and pour into the frosted glass and serve.

Alternative

Replace the blue curaçao and the triple sec with 1 measure of green curaçao or Galliano. To make a Frozen Margarita fill a glass with crushed ice and pour over the shaken cocktail.

Frozen Fruit Margarita

These are really simple to make and provide a delicious fruity drink, absolutely perfect for relaxing and having fun. Try experimenting with your favourite fruits and mixer liqueurs.

Ingredients   SERVES 1

1 measure freshly squeezed
    lemon juice
1 tbsp caster sugar
1$^{1}/_{2}$ measures tequila
1 measure strawberry liqueur
$^{1}/_{2}$ measure triple sec
3 ice cubes, crushed
1 fresh strawberry fan

Method

Frost the glass (see page 10) and allow it to dry. Place the tequila with the remaining lemon juice, strawberry liqueur and triple sec and add the crushed ice. Shake for 30 seconds or until blended then pour into the glass and serve garnished with the strawberry fan.

Alternative

Use Midori, Cointreau or Grand Marnier in place of the strawberry liqueur and garnish with the appropriate fruit.

Bazooka

Created in New Orleans around 1874, Southern Comfort was the result of a bartender, Wilkes Heron, wishing to improve the flavour of the harsh local brandy. He started adding other spirits as well as spices and other flavours. After much experimentation Southern Comfort was born; its recipe remains to this day a closely guarded secret.

Ingredients   SERVES 1

1 measure Southern Comfort
$^1/_2$ measure crème de banane
1 tsp grenadine
2 tbsp whipped cream
2 ice cubes
slice of banana and maraschino
    cherry to garnish

Method

Place the Southern Comfort into a cocktail shaker with the crème de banane and the grenadine. Add half the whipped cream and half the ice and shake for 30 seconds. Place the remaining ice into a short tumbler and strain over the shaken cocktail. Top with the remaining whipped cream and serve garnished with the fruit and a stirrer.

Caribbean Sunset

This cocktail is so named as the colours reflect not only the glorious sunsets in the Caribbean, but the flavour and aromas from the Islands.

Ingredients   SERVES 1

3 ice cubes

1 measure crème de banane

$1/2$ measure blue curaçao

$1/2$ measure freshly squeezed
   lemon juice

$1/2$ measure mango juice

2 tbsp whipped cream

1 tsp grenadine

slice of star fruit and a small wedge
   of mango to garnish

Method

Place a couple of the ice cubes into a cocktail shaker and the remaining ice into a short glass. Pour the crème de banane into the cocktail shaker together with the blue curaçao, the lemon and mango juice and half the whipped cream. Shake for 30 seconds or until blended. Pour over the ice cubes and add the grenadine allowing it to slowly sink. Top with the remaining cream, garnish and serve.

Alternative

Try adding $1/2$ measure of gin for more bite.

Calvados Cream

Calvados is an apple brandy that is made in Normandy, France, using fermented apple juice (cider) which is distilled and aged in oak casks. It is used in drinks and can be used in cooking.

Ingredients   SERVES 1

2 measures Calvados brandy

$^1/_2$ measure freshly squeezed
   lemon juice

1 tbsp very fresh organic egg white

2 tbsp double cream

1 tsp pineapple or sugar syrup (see
   page 10)

2 ice cubes, crushed (optional)

Sliced red apple to garnish

Method

Pour the Calvados brandy into a cocktail shaker together with the lemon juice, egg white, cream and pineapple or sugar syrup. Shake for 30 seconds or until blended. Place the crushed ice, if using, into a short tumbler then pour the cocktail and serve garnished with the apple slice.

Alternative

Use other brandies and garnishes in place of the Calvados, such as apricot brandy, garnish with an apricot slice or a cherry brandy with a fresh or maraschino cherry as a garnish.

Girl Scout

Baileys was the first Irish Cream Liqueur. It is a blend of Irish whiskey and cream and was introduced to the market in 1974. Although it contains no preservatives it has a shelf life of 2 years from the date of manufacturing and once opened should be used within six months.

Ingredients SERVES 1

2 ice cubes, crushed
$^1/_2$ measure schnapps
1 measure white crème de cacao
$^1/_2$ measure Baileys Irish Cream
1 tsp green crème de menthe
1 tbsp whipping cream
sprig of mint to garnish

Method

Place the schnapps into a cocktail shaker and add the crème de cacao, the Baileys and the crème de menthe. Add the whipping cream and shake for 20 seconds or until blended. Place the crushed ice into a short tumbler and pour over the cocktail. Garnish with the mint sprig and serve.

Mohican

One of the most well-known bourbons is from Kentucky – and goes under the colourful name of Wild Turkey. Bourbon is an American variation of whiskey and is to the States what Scotch whisky is to Scotland and Irish whiskey is to Ireland, all firmly stating that theirs is best.

Ingredients   SERVES 1

2 ice cubes
1¹/₂ measures white crème de cacao
1 measure bourbon
¹/₂ measure dry vermouth
1 measure whipping cream
¹/₂ tsp freshly grated plain
    dark chocolate

Method

Frost the glass (see page 10) and allow to dry. Place the white crème de cacao in a cocktail shaker and add the bourbon, dry vermouth and whipping cream. Add the ice and shake for 30 seconds or until blended. Strain into a cocktail glass (see page 9).

Alternative

Use one of the other whiskies available – try Canadian rye whiskey or Irish whiskey and see what the flavour difference is.

Southern Peach

This cocktail comes from the deep South of the USA and was created by Wilkes Heron of New Orleans who was responsible for developing Southern Comfort. This cocktail is one of the many that resulted from his trouble.

Ingredients   SERVES 1

1¹/₂ measures Southern Comfort
1¹/₂ measures peach brandy
1¹/₂ measures double cream
2 dashes Angostura Bitters
1 ice cube, crushed (optional)
peach slices to garnish

Method

Place the Southern Comfort into a cocktail shaker and add the peach brandy and double cream. Add the Angostura Bitters and crushed ice if using. Pour into a cocktail glass, garnish with the peach slices and serve.

Alternative

If liked, Orange Bitters can be used in place of the Angostura Bitters and the brandy could be replaced with Grand Marnier.

Orange Blossom

Gin is distilled from non–malted grain and the resulting spirit is flavoured with juniper berries and herbs. One of the largest areas for the growing of juniper berries is Umbria. It is mainly these berries that give gin its delicate aromatic flavour.

Ingredients   SERVES 1

1 ice cube
1 measure gin
1¹/₂ measures freshly squeezed
    orange juice
1 measure sweet rosso vermouth
1 tsp orange blossom honey, or use
    caster sugar
orange spiral to garnish

Method

Pour the gin, orange juice and sweet vermouth into a cocktail shaker and add the ice cube and orange blossom honey or sugar. Shake for 30 seconds or until blended then pour into a cocktail glass, garnish with the orange spiral, and serve.

Alternative

Replace the gin with peach brandy and garnish with peach slices to make a Peach Blossom.

Acapulco

This drink was originally made with dark rum, but due to travellers experiencing the delights of tequila in Mexico and other South American countries, tequila is instead the key ingredient.

Ingredients   SERVES 1

4 ice cubes, crushed

1 measure tequila

1 measure white rum

2 measures pineapple juice

1 measure freshly squeezed
  grapefruit juice

1 measure coconut milk

wedges of pineapple to garnish

Method

Place the ice cubes into a cocktail shaker and add the tequila, white rum, pineapple and grapefruit juice together with the coconut milk. Shake for 30 seconds then pour into a tall glass and serve garnished with wedges of pineapple.

Egg Nog

Originally the word 'nog' referred to a strong beer that was brewed in East Anglia. It was combined with egg and milk and drunk as a nourishing drink, but was more like a medicine as it was quite unpalatable. Over the years it has developed and is now very palatable, as the beer has been replaced with brandy.

Ingredients

SERVES 1

4 ice cubes
1 very fresh organic egg
1 tbsp sugar syrup (see page 10)
2 measures brandy
150 ml/¼ pt milk
freshly grated nutmeg to garnish

Method

Place the ice cubes into a cocktail shaker and add the egg, sugar syrup, brandy and milk. Shake for about 1 minute or until well blended then strain into a tall glass and serve sprinkled with freshly grated nutmeg.

Alternative

It is a question of personal choice as to which milk you use. If using full fat milk, the drink will be creamier than if you use either semi-skimmed or skimmed milk.

125

Pina Colada

This exotic cocktail originates In Puerto Rico and the name means 'strained pineapple juice'. You can use the pineapple juice from a can of pineapple or use fresh pineapple juice that will include the fruit fibres unless it is strained after blending in a liquidizer. Do make sure that the pineapple used is fresh and perfectly ripe. When served the whole drink should be milky white with no hint of separation.

Ingredients   SERVES 1

4 ice cubes, crushed

1 measure white rum

2 measures coconut cream

2 measures pineapple juice

pineapple wedge and maraschino
    cherry to garnish

Method

Place the crushed ice into a cocktail shaker and pour in the white rum, coconut cream and pineapple juice. Shake for 20 seconds or until well blended. Strain into a tall glass and garnish with the pineapple wedge and cherry and serve with a straw.

Alternative

Increase and decrease the amounts of rum and pineapple juice to taste.

Las Vegas

There are many myths and mysteries surrounding tequila and the drink that was originally only drunk by bandits – tequila is now enjoyed by all. Even the name is surrounded in mystery: it is said that it is an ancient Nahuati term meaning 'the plant of harvesting plants', but one thing is certain – it is a welcome addition to any bar.

Ingredients   SERVES 1

3 ice cubes
1 measure tequila
2 measures coconut cream
2 measures freshly squeezed
    orange juice
2 measures pineapple juice
1 measure whipped cream
pineapple wedge and maraschino
    cherry to garnish

Method

Place the ice into a cocktail shaker and pour in the tequila, coconut cream, orange and pineapple juice together with the cream. Shake for 20 seconds then strain into a tall tumbler and serve garnished with a pineapple wedge and cherry. Add a straw if liked.

Mai Tai

The Mai Tai was created by 'Trader Vic's' and over the years there has been much confusion concerning this cocktail. Originally it was a very strong rum–based drink with curaçao, orange, lime and sugar with grenadine added for colour. However, there have been many other versions served, many of which have been watered down with assorted and increased amounts of juice.

Ingredients   SERVES 1

3 ice cubes, crushed
lightly whisked egg white
1 tbsp caster sugar
$1^1/_2$ –2 measures dark rum
1 measure curaçao
$^1/_2$ measure grenadine
$^1/_2$ measure freshly squeezed
    orange juice
$^1/_2$ measure freshly squeezed
    lime juice
orange slice and pineapple wedge
    to garnish

Method

Frost the glass (see page 10) and once set carefully fill with the crushed ice. Pour the rum with the curaçao, grenadine and fruit juices into a cocktail shaker and shake for 30 seconds. Strain carefully over the crushed ice and serve garnished with the orange slice and pineapple wedge.

Frozen Key Lime

This could almost be regarded as a cross between a dessert and a drink as it is based on the very popular pudding – Key Lime Pie. Beware, the dessert does not have a kick like this has. Enjoy.

Ingredients
SERVES 1

3 ice cubes

1 measure white rum

$^1/_2$ measure dark rum

$1^1/_2$ measures freshly squeezed
   lime juice

1–2 scoops good quality vanilla
   ice cream

soda water to top up

little grated chocolate to garnish

Method

Place the ice into a cocktail shaker
and pour in the white and dark rum
together with the lime juice. Shake
for 30 seconds or until blended then
strain into a tall glass and top up
with the soda water. Float the ice
cream on top. Sprinkle with the
grated chocolate. Serve with a
straw and spoon if liked.

Alternative
Use a mixture of citrus fruit juices
rather than the lime juice and
garnish with a twist from each.

Tobago Fizz

When using citrus fruits for their juice there are a couple of tricks that are both quick and easy that will help to get the maximum amount of juice from the fruits. Either roll the fruit on a work surface for a couple of minutes before attempting to squeeze or heat for 30–40 seconds in a microwave, cool then squeeze. Either way you will get far more juice from the fruits.

Ingredients   SERVES 1

4 ice cubes
1 tbsp freshly squeezed lime juice
2 tbsp freshly squeezed orange juice
3 measures golden or white rum
1 measure single cream
$^1/_2$ tsp clear honey
soda water to top up
strawberry to garnish

Method

Place the ice cubes into a cocktail shaker and pour in the lime and orange juice. Add the rum with the single cream and honey. Shake for 45 seconds or until a frost forms on the outside of the cocktail shaker. Strain into a tall stemmed glass and serve garnished with a strawberry.

Florida Keys

Passion fruits are ready for use once they are very wrinkled and the outside skin has begun to cave in. It is not worth using them before as the flavour and aroma will not have developed.

Ingredients   SERVES 1

4 ice cubes, crushed
2 measures white rum
1 measure freshly squeezed lime juice
1 ripe passion fruit
1 measure double cream
redcurrant sprig (if available) and
    orange slice to garnish

Method

Place the ice cubes into a cocktail shaker and add the white rum and lime juice. Scoop out the pulp and seeds with the juice from the passion fruit and add to the shaker together with the double cream. Shake for 45 seconds or until a frost forms on the outside of the shaker. Pour into a hurricane glass (see page 9) and garnish with the redcurrant sprig if using and orange slice.

Alternative

Replace the lime juice and passion fruit with all orange juice. Use 2$^1\!/_2$ measures of freshly squeezed orange juice and strain into the glass.

131

Long Island Iced Tea

A hangover is almost guaranteed with just one of these cocktails. It dates back to Prohibition and was originally made with any spirit that was available at that time, which most probably accounts for all the different recipes that are around.

Ingredients SERVES 1

4–6 ice cubes
$^1/_2$ measure white rum
$^1/_2$ measure vodka
$^1/_2$ measure gin
$^1/_2$ measure tequila
$^1/_2$ measure Cointreau
$^1/_2$ measure triple sec
1 measure freshly squeezed
    lime juice
$^1/_2$ measure sugar syrup (see page 10)
4 measures cola to top up
orange twist to garnish

Method

Place the ice cubes into a tall glass and pour in the rum, vodka, gin, tequila, Cointreau and triple sec. Stir with a bar spoon then add the lime juice and top up with the cola. Serve with a stirrer and garnish with the orange twist.

Alternative

If liked omit the tequila and triple sec and add 1 measure blue curaçao.

Cocobanana

This delicious exotic cocktail takes its name from where it originated and of course the ingredients used. A perfect cocktail to enjoy when the weather is hot and sunny and the going is tough. It is the ideal way to wind down and chill out.

Ingredients   SERVES 1

3 ice cubes
1 measure white rum
1 measure crème de banane
$^1/_2$ measure amaretto liqueur
1–1$^1/_2$ measures coconut rum
3 measures pineapple juice
1 measure coconut cream
$^1/_2$ a ripe banana
2 scoops good quality vanilla
   ice cream
wedge of pineapple, orange slice
   and banana slice to garnish

Method

Place the ice into a cocktail shaker then pour in the white rum, crème de banane, amaretto, coconut rum, pineapple juice and coconut cream. Mash the banana and add to the cocktail shaker together with the ice cream. Shake for 1 minute or until blended then pour into a tall glass and serve with a spoon and straw garnished with the fruit.

Alternative

If liked, place the ingredients into a blender and whizz for 20 seconds before straining into the glass.

Chocolate Monkey

This cocktail is definitely for the chocoholics and if liked you can increase the amount of chocolate used. Chocolate and rum are the perfect combination and when cream is added the result is sublime.

Ingredients SERVES 1

1 tbsp finely grated plain chocolate

3 ice cubes, crushed

1 measure crème de banane

1 measure white rum

$^1/_2$–1 measure chocolate syrup

$^1/_2$ ripe banana

2 tbsp double cream, lightly whipped

banana slices and strawberry
   to garnish

Method

Frost the glass (see page 10) with chocolate and allow it to dry. Place the crushed ice into a blender with the crème de banane, rum and chocolate syrup. Slice the banana and add to the blender. Whiz for 20–30 seconds then pour into a tall glass and float the cream on top. Sprinkle the top with grated chocolate to taste and serve with a straw and spoon garnished with the fruit.

Alternative

The cocktail can be made using a cocktail shaker if liked. Simply place all the ingredients into the shaker and shake for 45 seconds or until blended. Pour into the glass, float with the cream, garnish and serve.

Island Affair

Mango is a large tropical fruit that is growing in popularity throughout the world. It does need to be eaten when ripe otherwise the delicious flavour will not have developed. Allow to ripen at room temperature before using and once ripe, store in the vegetable compartment of the refrigerator, but allow it to come to room temperature before using.

Ingredients   SERVES 1

3 ice cubes, crushed
1 measure Midori (melon liqueur)
1–1¹/₂ measures Cointreau
¹/₂ measure blue curaçao
1¹/₂ measures freshly squeezed
    orange juice
2 measures mango juice
1 tbsp lightly whipped cream
mango slice, pineapple slice and
    melon wedge to garnish

Method

Place the crushed ice into a tall glass. Pour the Midori into a cocktail shaker together with the Cointreau, blue curaçao and the fruit juices. Shake for 30 seconds or until blended then strain over the crushed ice. Float the whipped cream on top and serve garnished with the fruits and with a straw and spoon.

Lazy Daze

Crème de menthe is a peppermint or spearmint flavoured liqueur and is available in either green or clear (referred to as white). Both varieties are interchangeable unless the colour is crucial to the finished drink or dish. It can be served over ice as a digestive or combined with other ingredients to give a refreshing hint of mint. In some instances it is also added to food.

Ingredients   SERVES 1

3 ice cubes, crushed
1 measure vodka
1 measure Kahlúa
$^1/_2$ measure green crème de menthe
2 measures lemonade
1 tbsp whipped cream
mint sprig to garnish

Method

Place the crushed ice into a tall glass. Pour the vodka into a cocktail shaker with the Kahlúa liqueur and crème de menthe. Shake for 20 seconds then pour into the ice-filled glass. Top up with the lemonade. Float the cream on top and garnish with a mint sprig.

Love in the Afternoon

Many of the strawberry liqueurs (crèmes de fraises) contain not only the everyday varieties of strawberries that we are all familiar with but also the very delicate wild strawberry. Made in countries as diverse as France and Australia this modern liqueur is becoming very popular.

Ingredients   SERVES 1

2 measures dark rum

$^1/_2$ measure strawberry liqueur

1 measure freshly squeezed
    orange juice

$^1/_2$ measure coconut cream

2 tsp sugar syrup (see page 10)

4 ripe strawberries, lightly rinsed

Method

Place the rum with the strawberry liqueur, orange juice, coconut cream and the sugar syrup into a blender. Reserve one of the strawberries to use as a garnish, slice the remainder and add to the blender. Whizz for 20 seconds or until smooth then add the crushed ice. Whizz again for a further 20 seconds then pour into a tall glass and serve with a stirrer and garnish with the reserved strawberry.

Alternative

For a richer cocktail, add $^1/_2$ measure of double cream in addition to the coconut cream.

Cups and Punches

It is unclear where the word 'Punch' originated from. There are some who think it comes from the word 'Puncheon', which is a cask designed to hold liquids. So it is easy to see how a punchbowl could easily have been made from a small part of the Puncheon and the drink in the bowl called 'Punch'.

However, another school of thought is that the word comes from the Indian word 'panch' or the Persian word 'pani', both meaning 'five'. This ties in with the original punches, which were made from just five ingredients. The five basic ingredients then reflected the five elements – sweet, sour, bitter, alcohol and a weak liquid to provide the bulk of the drink.

Many believe that it was the British sailors who first discovered Punch in India around the sixteenth century. In addition the first recorded British document that mentions 'Punches' was around 1632.

Towards the end of the fifteenth century, Punch houses were springing up. Originally punches were made in the same way as today's 'Wassail Bowl' and made from ale, brandy or wine. However with the exploration of Jamaica, and the discovery of rum, 'Punches' began to increase in popularity and variation.

Cups are traditionally English and were originally offered to huntsmen before departing on a hunt. Cups are normally not as alcoholic as Punches and are made from wine and low alcoholic spirits such as sloe gin. Whatever your preference – 'Punches' or 'Cups' – they will help any gathering go with a swing.

Classic Pimm's

This is one of the most well-known and much loved Punch of all. Pimm's is gin-based and although its recipe is a closely guarded secret it is possible to detect subtle aromas of spices and citrus fruits. There are five other Pimm's available and the main difference is the base alcohol used.

Ingredients   SERVES 1

30 cl/10 fl oz Pimm's No. 1
70 cl/23$^{1}/_{2}$ fl oz lemonade
small piece cucumber, thinly sliced
$^{1}/_{2}$ orange, thinly sliced and each
    slice cut in half
$^{1}/_{2}$ red or green apple, cored
    and sliced
6 strawberries, lightly rinsed and
    sliced if large
2–3 sprigs borage or mint
10–12 ice cubes

Method

Pour the Pimm's into a large glass serving jug and add the ice cubes, the cucumber and prepared fruits. Stir well before adding the borage or mint sprigs. Leave for the flavours to infuse, at least 10 minutes, then serve in tall glasses with spoons.

Alternative

When wishing to serve a single glass of Pimm's, use one measure of Pimm's to one measure of lemonade or soda water. Use as much or as little fruit as preferred.

Wassail Bowl

This is one of the very first 'Punches' that has been recorded and dates back to the fifteenth century. The original recipe consisted of just three ingredients – ale, brandy and a little spice. Time however has moved on and now there are many variations, most of which produce a far more alcoholic beverage.

Ingredients

SERVES 12

6–8 eating apples
2.25 litres/4 pts ale
75 g/3 oz white sugar
15 cl sweet sherry
1 tsp freshly grated nutmeg
5 cm/2 in piece root ginger, grated

Method

Core the apples and place on a baking tray. Cook in a preheated oven (200°C/fan oven 180°C/Gas 6) for 35–40 minutes or until soft. Remove and keep warm. Pour the ale into a saucepan and stir in the sugar and the sherry. Sprinkle in the nutmeg and add the root ginger. Heat, stirring until the sugar has dissolved. Place the apples into individual cups and pour over the hot ale. Serve while still hot with spoons so you can eat the apple.

Champagne Punch

You may wonder which glass to use when serving a Champagne Punch – should it be a flute or a coupe or a punch glass? The type of glass has often been dictated by fashion but really it should be whichever makes the drink taste the best. For a Punch, because the champagne is mixed with other ingredients, a punch glass or coupe glass (see page 9) seems best.

Ingredients   SERVES 14

10–12 small ice cubes to serve
175 g/6 oz caster sugar
3 measures brandy
3 measures triple sec
2 measures maraschino syrup from a
   jar of cherries
1 bottle chilled freshly opened
   champagne
1 litre chilled sparkling water
100 g/4 oz mixed summer berries,
   lightly rinsed, and sliced if large

Method

Spoon the sugar into a large bowl or punchbowl and pour in the brandy and triple sec. Stir until the sugar has completely dissolved then stir in the maraschino syrup. Add the champagne with the sparkling water and the ice cubes, stir then ladle into champagne glasses.

Alternative

Replace the chilled sparkling water with lemonade for a sweeter Punch. Cava or sparkling wine could be used in place of the champagne; try pink sparkling wine.

Boston Punch

It is well worth investing in a punchbowl complete with the glasses and ladle if you frequently throw parties. Just the look of the bowl will lift any table and reflect a real party atmosphere.

Ingredients   SERVES 12–14

1 tbsp white sugar
14 cl/4¾ fl oz brandy
3 measures triple sec
3 measures dark rum
4 measures freshly squeezed lemon juice
28 cl/9½ fl oz dry cider
1 bottle freshly opened chilled champagne
40 cl/13½ fl oz sparkling water
thin slices of red and green apple to garnish

Method

Sprinkle the sugar into a punchbowl and pour in the brandy. Stir until the sugar has dissolved. Then stir in the triple sec, rum and the lemon juice. Slowly stir in the cider and then the champagne and water. Add the apple and serve ensuring that everyone gets 1–2 slices of apple.

El Grito

Every year on the 16th September, there is much rejoicing as all Mexicans celebrate El Grito. This is when they celebrate Mexico's independence from Spanish rule. So raise a glass and join in the festivities.

Ingredients   SERVES 8

8–10 ice cubes, crushed
350 g/12 oz fresh ripe strawberries
2 tbsp clear honey
70 cl tequila

Method

Reserve a few strawberries for decoration then hull and lightly rinse the remainder. Place in a food processor and add the honey. Blend for 2 minutes or until a purée is formed. Scrape into a bowl and chill until required. Pour the tequila into a punchbowl and stir in the strawberry purée. Add sufficient crushed ice to give a 'slushy' texture. Ladle into glasses and decorate with fresh strawberries.

Alternative
Use sugar syrup in place of the honey. Add to taste.

Sangria

There can be nothing better than sitting in the hot sun on a Spanish terrace or beach, sipping a glass or two of Sangria while watching the world go by. It even works at home as long as the weather is hot and sunny.

Ingredients   SERVES 12

8 ice cubes, crushed
$^1/_2$ apple, cored and sliced
$^1/_2$ orange cut into small wedges
$^1/_2$ lemon cut into small slices
6 strawberries, sliced
1 bottle 75 cl Spanish red wine
    such as Rioja
4 measures Spanish brandy
1 large orange
1 large ripe lemon
20 cl/6$^3/_4$ fl oz soda water or
    lemonade

Method

Place the chopped up fruit into a large serving jug or punchbowl and pour in the red wine. Stir in the brandy. Squeeze the juice from the orange and lemon and stir into the wine and brandy together with the soda water or lemonade.

Add the ice and serve with a large spoon to enable stirring and the fruit to be placed into the glasses and, if liked, straws.

Alternative

Try using rosé wine in place of the red wine and a little honey if a sweeter drink is preferred.

Rosy Punch

Rosé or blush wines are sometimes referred to as summertime wines, but are rapidly growing in popularity the whole year round. They are produced in France, Italy, Spain and Portugal as well as the New World countries and there is bound to be a wine to suit every taste.

Ingredients   SERVES 14–16

10 ice cubes
2 x 75 cl/25$^1/_3$ fl oz chilled rosé wine
6 measures brandy
150 ml/$^1/_4$ pt raspberry syrup
2 splits (each 200 ml/7 fl oz)
    tonic water
1 lemon, preferably organic, thinly
    sliced and cut into half moons

Method

Pour the rosé wine into a punchbowl and stir in the brandy and raspberry syrup. Stir well then add the tonic water and the lemon half moon slices, and ice cubes.

Alternative

If liked make your own raspberry syrup. Lightly rinse 300 g/10 oz fresh or frozen raspberries, place in a heavy-based saucepan and add 50 g/2 oz sugar and 2 tablespoons of water. Place over a gentle heat and cook for 10 minutes or until the fruit has collapsed. Cool then pass through a food processor and rub through a fine sieve to remove any seeds. Store in a screw top jar in the refrigerator for up to 1 week.

Creole Punch

When making a Punch to serve it is always a good idea to have some extra 'mixers' such as lemonade, soda or tonic water to add to the Punch in case it is too strong.

Ingredients   SERVES 10–12

12 ice cubes, crushed
1 bottle port
6 measures (or to taste) brandy
3 measures freshly squeezed
    lemon juice
lemonade to top up
orange and lemon half moon and
    kiwi slice to garnish

Method

Place the crushed ice into a tall glass and pour over the port and brandy. Add the lemon juice then stir well and top up with the lemonade. Spear the orange, lemon and kiwi slices on to a cocktail stick and serve with a stirrer and straw.

Alternative

Make a single glass in the same method and using the following amounts: 4 ice cubes, crushed; 2 measures port; $^{1}/_{2}$ measure brandy and 2 tsp freshly squeezed lemon juice. Garnish as above.

Knockout Punch

Cider is made mainly from specially grown varieties of apple and generally has a strong alcoholic content (over 5%), is yellow in colour and often cloudy. Much of the UK cider is grown in the South West.

Ingredients   SERVES 12

1 litre/ 1$^1/_2$ pts medium dry cider
2–3 measures gin
2–3 measures brandy
2 measures peach schnapps or use
   extra brandy
2–3 tbsp clear honey (optional)
2 ripe peaches, stoned, sliced
   or chopped
30 cl/10 fl oz lemonade

Method

Pour the cider into a punchbowl and stir in the gin, brandy and peach schnapps or extra brandy. Add the clear honey to taste and the sliced or chopped peaches. Chill for up to 2 hours. When ready stir in the lemonade then serve.

Alternative

You may see some Knockout Punches made with tequila and rum.

Claret Cup

It may seem unusual to use a claret and then to serve it chilled. In fact if you lived in France this would not be at all unusual as in the summer months red wine is frequently served slightly chilled. It is delicious and perfect for a warm summer evening. Try it and see.

Ingredients   SERVES 8–10

4 tbsp sugar syrup (see page 10)
1 lemon, preferably organic
2 small oranges, preferably organic
2 measures brandy
1 bottle claret
2 splits (each 200 ml/7 fl oz)
    tonic water
2–3 sprigs of borage if available
thin slices from $^1/_2$ orange and
    $^1/_2$ lemon

Method

Place the sugar syrup into a heavy–based saucepan. Thinly peel the rind from the lemon and oranges and squeeze out the juice. Add the peel to the sugar syrup and bring to the boil, reduce the heat and simmer very gently for 10 minutes. Remove and allow it to cool then strain, discarding the peel. Stir the strained syrup and the lemon and orange juice into a punchbowl then stir in the claret. Chill for up to 1 hour before floating the borage on top and garnishing with the fruit slices.

Honeysuckle Cup

When choosing wine to use in a Cup or Punch it is always a good idea to use a reasonably good wine. Using cheap inferior wine in the end can cost you more money as you could either spend time and money trying to improve the finished result or you may end up disappointed.

Ingredients   SERVES 12

8 ice cubes, crushed

1 bottle medium dry white wine,
    such as a chardonnay

1 tbsp clear honey

2 measures brandy

600 ml/1 pt lemonade

1 ripe peach, stoned, sliced
    and chopped

50 g/2 oz lightly rinsed
    strawberries, sliced

Method

Pour the wine into a punchbowl and
stir in the honey and brandy. Stir
until the honey has completely
dissolved then stir in the lemonade,
sliced fruits and crushed ice.
Leave to stand for 30 minutes
before serving.

Midsummer Night's Dream

This Cup is absolutely delightful and the perfect drink to offer in the summer, either during the day or evening. Try using borage if available or a few mint sprigs or even a little lemon balm.

Ingredients   SERVES 16–18

1 bottle white wine such as Riesling

1 bottle red wine such as Beaujolais

2 measures Cointreau

2–3 tbsp clear honey

1 slice gallia melon

1 ripe peach

10 ripe strawberries

10 ice cubes, crushed

600 ml/1 pt lemonade

few fresh herbs

Method

Pour all the wine into a punchbowl and stir in the Cointreau and honey. Stir until the honey has completely dissolved. Discard the skin and seeds from the melon then dice into small pieces. Lightly rinse the peach, cut in half and discard the stone. Chop and add to the bowl together with the ice and then the lemonade and herbs. Stir, then leave for 30 minutes to allow the flavours to develop before serving.

Alternative

Use a variety of different fruits according to availability and preference. Try mixed summer berries, fresh cherries or even apples, pears and fresh blackberries.

Hot Spicy Cider

In order to get the maximum flavour from the cinnamon sticks it is important that they are lightly bruised. Simply wrap then in either a piece of cling film or kitchen paper and bash lightly with a rolling pin or meat mallet. Use as directed.

Ingredients   SERVES 8

1.2 litres/2 pts dry cider

50–75 g/2–3 oz or to taste golden
    granulated sugar

6 whole cloves

2 cinnamon sticks, lightly bruised

3 star anise fruits

1 small orange, thinly sliced and cut
    into half moons.

Method

Pour the cider into a heavy-based saucepan and place over a medium heat. Add the sugar together with the whole cloves, the cinnamon sticks and the star anise. Cut the orange into thin slices and cut each slice in half. Add to the saucepan then heat gently, stirring frequently until the sugar has completely dissolved. Strain into heatproof glasses or tumblers and serve with 1–2 half moon orange slices.

Glühwein

A drink that is synonymous with skiing and 'après ski', a wonderful warming aromatic drink that is perfect for any cold evening, it is too good to leave it for 'après ski' — enjoy it any time.

Ingredients   SERVES 8

600 ml/1 pt red wine such as Burgundy

50 g/2 oz light muscovado sugar

4 whole cloves

2 cinnamon sticks, lightly bruised

1 tsp whole allspice

1 lemon, thinly sliced, preferably
   organic

4 measures brandy

Method

Pour the wine into a heavy-based saucepan and stir in the sugar. Add the cloves, cinnamon sticks and the allspice. Heat gently, stirring frequently until the sugar has melted. Cut the lemon slices into half moons then add to the saucepan. Heat gently for about 15–20 minutes or until it is just below boiling point. Add the brandy and heat gently for a further 5 minutes. Strain into heatproof glasses and serve.

Alternative

Wrap the spices into a small piece of muslin rather than just placing them in the wine and sugar. This will make their removal far easier and there is no need to strain.

Christmas Wine

This is a fantastic drink to enjoy by the fire at Christmas time. The alcohol–soaked raisins take on so much flavour that they add another dimension to the drinking experience.

Ingredients   SERVES 12

35 cl /1¹/₂ bottle gin
1 bottle red wine, such as Burgundy
75 g/3 oz seedless raisins
50 g/2 oz light muscovado sugar
6 green cardamom pods,
   lightly cracked
3 whole cloves
1 cinnamon stick, lightly bruised
thinly pared rind from ¹/₂ lemon

Method

Pour the gin and red wine into a heavy–based saucepan and add the raisins and sugar. Tie the spices and lemon rind into a small square of muslin and add to the saucepan. Heat gently, stirring frequently for 12–15 minutes then bring to just below boiling point. Stir occasionally. Remove the muslin bag of spices then ladle into heatproof glasses and serve.

Funchal Cup

Heating wine with a spirit and sugar often increases the effect of the drink for many people. Take care when drinking a cup of hot Punch especially if you are not used to hot punches.

Ingredients   SERVES 18–20

1 bottle Madeira
2 measures brandy
4 measures apricot brandy
4 measures kirsch
600 ml/1 pt freshly squeezed
    orange juice
1 cinnamon stick, lightly bruised
300 ml/$^1/_2$ pt water
50 g/2 oz (or to taste) light
    muscovado sugar

Method

Pour the Madeira and both brandies into a heavy-based saucepan and add the kirsch together with the orange juice and cinnamon stick. Stir in the water and sugar then place over a gentle heat. Bring slowly to just below boiling point, stirring frequently until the sugar has completely dissolved. Check for sweetness (adding more sugar if preferred) and for the alcoholic strength. Add more water if liked and heat gently until hot. Serve in heatproof glasses.

Alternative

Serve with a long cinnamon stick to use as a stirrer. Or omit some of the sugar and serve with a sugar swizzle stick.

Mulled Ale

In the fifteenth and sixteenth centuries ale was the common drink as water was far too toxic. Tea and coffee were almost unheard of as were fruit juices so ale and wine were commonplace. To make ale more palatable for some, spices were added that greatly enhanced the flavour especially when served warm. The recipe below is a modern version of the idea of spicing up ale.

Ingredients

SERVES 8–10

1 lemon, preferably organic
$\frac{1}{2}$ tsp freshly grated nutmeg
$\frac{1}{4}$ tsp ground cinnamon
25 g/1 oz demerara sugar
300 ml/$\frac{1}{2}$ pt water
600 ml/1 pt ale
3 measures brandy
1 measure rum
1 measure gin

Method

Thinly pare the rind from the lemon and place in a heatproof saucepan. Sprinkle in the freshly grated nutmeg and cinnamon then stir in the sugar and water. Squeeze out the juice from the lemon and strain into the saucepan. Place over a gentle heat and bring to the boil, stirring. When the sugar has dissolved stir in the ale, brandy, rum and gin. Heat gently for 12–15 minutes or until hot, but not boiling. Ladle into heatproof glasses and serve.

The Bishop

This traditional recipe is often served around Christmas time. The nineteenth–century cookery writer Eliza Acton has been credited with the development of this punch and Charles Dickens also mentions it in some of his novels. It can also be called The Smoking Bishop.

Ingredients   SERVES 12–14

1 lemon, preferably organic
12 whole cloves
1¹/₂ bottles ruby port
600 ml/1 pt water
50 g/2 oz golden granulated sugar
1 tsp ground mixed spice
cinnamon sticks for stirring

Method

Preheat the oven to 180°C/(fan oven) 160°C/Gas 4. Stick the whole cloves into the lemon then roast in the oven for 30 minutes. Remove and place in a heatproof bowl. Pour in the port with the water and sugar and sprinkle in the mixed spices. Place over a saucepan of gently simmering water and heat for 30 minutes or until very hot. Serve hot with cinnamon stick stirrers.

Alternative

Try roasting an orange rather than a lemon.

Bahamas Punch

Rum is made from distilling fermented sugar and water. The sugar comes from sugar cane and is fermented from cane juice. Concentrated cane juice or molasses is the sweet sticky residue that remains after the sugar has been extracted and the juice boiled off. The molasses is used with minerals and other trace elements to make rum.

Ingredients   SERVES 12

100 g/4 oz (or to taste) light
    muscovado sugar
300 ml/ $^1/_2$ pt water
1 lemon, preferably organic
3 small oranges, preferably organic
300 ml/ $^1/_2$ pt cold strong black tea
70 cl dark rum
small wedge fresh pineapple
orange spiral

Method

Place the sugar into a heatproof saucepan and pour in the water. Thinly pare the rind from the lemon and one of the oranges and add to the saucepan. Heat gently, stirring frequently for 12–15 minutes or until the sugar has dissolved. Bring to the boil, and boil for 5 minutes then remove from the heat. Squeeze out the juice from all the fruits and add to the saucepan together with the tea and rum. Stir, then strain into heatproof glasses and serve garnished with an orange spiral and a wedge of pineapple.

Summer Cup

When using clear honey it is not always easy to measure accurately. There are two good ways that work every time. Heat a measuring spoon in very hot water, dip into the honey and scoop out the amount. Or heat the jar for 30 seconds in the microwave then measure.

Ingredients   SERVES 12–14

8 ice cubes, crushed
1 bottle sparkling white wine
3 measures white rum
2 measures freshly squeezed
    orange juice
3 measures freshly squeezed
    lemon juice
4 measures pineapple juice
2 tbsp clear honey (or to taste)
300 ml/ $^1/_2$ pt ginger ale
25 g/1 oz fresh raspberries, 1 peach
    and 2–3 mint sprigs to garnish

Method

Pour the sparkling wine into a punchbowl and stir in the rum with the strained fruit juices. Add the honey and stir until dissolved then add the crushed ice and the ginger ale. Lightly rinse the raspberries, slice the peach and cut into small pieces. Add to the punch together with the mint sprigs and serve.

Alternative

For a fruity cup, replace the ginger ale with the same amount of freshly brewed fruit tea, leave to cool then add to the bowl.

Apple Cider Cup

When using the rind from the citrus fruits it is always a good idea to scrub thoroughly.
This will remove any wax, pesticides or fertilizers that may be present.

Ingredients   SERVES 12

2 dessert apples
1 lemon, preferably organic
8 whole cloves
4 tbsp sugar syrup (see page 10)
1.5 litres/2$^1/_2$ pts medium dry cider
300 ml/$^1/_2$ pt soda water

Method

Cut the apples into quarters and
core then thinly slice and place in a
heatproof bowl. Thinly pare the rind
from the lemon and add to the bowl
together with the strained juice
from the lemon. Add the whole
cloves. Heat the sugar syrup to just
below boiling point then pour over
the apples. Leave to cool. Carefully
pour in the cider together with the
soda water, and serve.

Alternative
Serve with ice if liked.

Tropical Cup

The Caribbean is the home of rum and every island produces their own brand. Rum is also produced in Barbados, Cuba, the Dominican Republic, Guyana, Haiti, Jamaica and Martinique, all creating their own special, closely-guarded recipe.

Ingredients   SERVES 16

10 ice cubes, crushed

30 cl/10 fl oz dark rum

25 cl/8½ fl oz apricot brandy

30 cl/10 fl oz pineapple juice

30 cl/10 fl oz freshly squeezed pink
    grapefruit juice

15 cl/5 fl oz freshly squeezed
    orange juice

20 cl/6¾ fl oz mango juice

3 ripe passion fruits

1 small ripe mango and 12–16
    maraschino cherries to garnish

Method

Pour the rum and brandy into a punchbowl and stir in all the fruit juices. Scoop out the flesh, seeds and juice from the passion fruits and stir into the bowl together with the crushed ice. Peel and stone the mango then cut into small dice and stir into the punch together with the maraschino cherries. Serve.

Dr Johnson's Choice

It is widely believed that this Punch was the favourite tipple of and was named after Dr Samuel Johnson who was responsible for his 'Dictionary of the English Language'.

Ingredients

SERVES 10–12

1 bottle red wine, such as a Merlot

12 sugar lumps

6 whole cloves

600 ml/1 pt boiling water

4 measures curaçao

4 measures brandy

freshly grated nutmeg

Method

Pour the wine into a heavy-based saucepan and add the sugar lumps and whole cloves. Place over a gentle heat and bring to just below boiling point. Add the boiling water together with the curaçao and brandy. Pour into heatproof glasses and serve with a little freshly grated nutmeg on top.

Bacardi and Champagne Punch

It was in the early nineteenth century that Don Facundo Bacardi Masso, a winemaker, attempted to 'tame' rum. He made several attempts to refine the flavour and finally filtered the alcohol through charcoal, which removed many of the impurities. By ageing the rum in oak barrels, it mellowed to become 'white' or clear rum, that now constitutes what we know as Bacardi rum.

Ingredients   SERVES 16

20 cl/6¾ fl oz white Bacardi rum

5 measures triple sec

5 measures amaretto liqueur

2 measures grenadine

3 measures sugar syrup (see page 10)

1 small pineapple

1 bottle champagne, chilled

600 ml/1 pt sparkling water, chilled

Method

Pour the Bacardi white rum into a punchbowl and stir in the triple sec, amaretto liqueur, grenadine and sugar syrup. Stir. Discard the plume, skin and hard central core from the pineapple and cut the fruit into small wedges. Add to the punchbowl, cover lightly and chill for at least 2 hours. When ready to serve, stir in the chilled champagne and the sparkling water and serve.

Alternative

To lessen the alcoholic impact of this drink try substituting the triple sec or liqueur with apricot or guava nectar.

Non-Alcoholic Cocktails

There is, as the expression goes, 'a time and a place', and sometimes serving an alcoholic drink is neither required nor the correct thing to do. As long as they are delicious-looking and taste divine, a non-alcoholic drink can give as much pleasure as any alcoholic one.

When throwing a party remember that often some of the guests will be driving and it would be quite wrong to encourage the drivers to drink alcohol. If offered a stunning cocktail that is alcohol free, they will enjoy the party or occasion as much as anybody.

When preparing alcohol free drinks the same care and attention should be paid to all the details. Use freshly squeezed juices wherever possible, as these will give the maximum flavour. Use the juices up quickly; do not be tempted to keep the juice for days. Sometimes you may find that the juices have either a very acidic tang or are full of fibre. If the former is the case, adjust by the use of extra sweetness, using either honey or sugar and if full of fibre, sieve before using.

Do use attractive garnishes; do not be tempted to skimp for, as with food, a drink should appeal to all the senses, so should look inviting as well as have a good aroma and taste. This chapter has a broad appeal and will ensure that all of your guests benefit from and contribute to the party atmosphere.

Virgin Mary

As the name suggests this is the alcohol free version of a 'Bloody Mary'. When poured into the glass, garnished with the celery stick and with the dash or two of Worcestershire sauce, it looks as good as any cocktail.

Ingredients   SERVES 1

4 ice cubes
5 measures tomato juice
$^1/_2$–1 tsp Tabasco
1–2 dashes Worcestershire sauce
1 tsp freshly squeezed lemon juice
celery stick and lemon twist
   to garnish

Method

Place the ice cubes into a short tumbler and pour over the tomato juice. Add the Tabasco to taste together with the Worcestershire sauce and lemon juice. Stir well until mixed then serve garnished with the celery stick and lemon twist.

Alternative

If liked make this a tall drink. Half fill a tall glass with crushed ice and pour in the tomato juice. Add the Tabasco and Worcestershire sauce to taste together with the lemon juice and top up with soda water. Use the celery stick as the stirrer.

Strawberry Kiss

If the strawberries that you are using are not that ripe, slice and sprinkle with either a little freshly ground black pepper or balsamic vinegar. Leave for 1–2 hours then use as directed. The strawberries can also be heated briefly in a microwave; this will help the flavour immensely.

Ingredients   SERVES 1

3 ice cubes, crushed

3 measures strawberry purée

1¹/₂ measures freshly squeezed
    orange juice

1 measure freshly squeezed
    lemon juice

3–4 measures lemonade

1 tbsp whipped cream

sprinkle freshly grated chocolate

1 fanned strawberry to garnish

Method

Place the strawberry purée into a cocktail shaker or jug and add the orange and lemon juice. Shake for 20 seconds or until blended. If using a jug, stir vigorously until thoroughly blended. Place the crushed ice into a tumbler and pour over the strawberry mixture. Top up with the lemonade and float the whipped cream on top. Sprinkle the cream with the chocolate and garnish with a fanned strawberry. Serve with a straw.

Alternative

Try using other flavoured fruit purée; try raspberry, a mixture of berries, mango or papaya.

Hawaiian Island Surfer

Part of the pleasure of a drink, especially at a party, is its look. The garnish should reflect the flavours of the drink itself. Here the tropical feel is echoed in the use of wedges of papaya and pineapple.

Ingredients
SERVES 1

2 measures tropical fruit juice

1 measure coconut cream

3 scoops lemon sorbet (or water ice)

4 measures ginger ale

papaya and pineapple wedges and
   maraschino cherry to garnish

Method

Place the tropical fruit juice into a chilled tumbler and stir in the coconut cream. Add scoops of lemon sorbet (or water ice) and top up with the ginger ale. Thread the fruits on a cocktail stick to garnish and place across the glass. Serve.

Alternative

Use pineapple juice, rather than 'tropical' juice, if preferred.

Virgin Raspberry Daiquiri

Alcohol free cocktails are the perfect answer for underage teenagers. Serve a selection to them, beautifully garnished with straws, umbrellas and pieces of fruit and wow them all.

Ingredients   SERVES 1

4 ice cubes, crushed

1 tsp caster sugar

3 measures raspberry syrup or fresh
fruit purée

2 measures pineapple juice

$1/2$ measure lemon juice

lemonade to top up

fresh raspberries threaded on to a
cocktail stick and mint sprig
to garnish

Method

Place the caster sugar into a saucer and place some water in another saucer. Dip the rim of a chilled glass into the water and then into the sugar. Turn the rim until well coated in the sugar then chill until required. Pour the raspberry syrup or fresh fruit purée into a cocktail shaker or jug and add the pineapple and lemon juice. Shake or stir until well blended. Place the crushed ice into the sugared glass and pour over the blended drink. Top up with lemonade and serve garnished with fresh raspberries and mint sprig.

Southern Ginger

This tangy drink is perfect for hot sunny days and will certainly help to keep the temperature down. It is a good idea to chill the lemonade beforehand and once it is opened remember to keep the bottle tightly screwed down, so as to keep the fizz in.

Ingredients   SERVES 1

3 ice cubes, crushed

5 measures dry ginger ale

1 measure freshly squeezed
    lemon juice

$1/2$–1 tsp sugar syrup (see page 10)

lemonade to top up

mint sprig to garnish

Method

Place the dry ginger ale into a tumbler and stir in the lemon juice and sugar syrup to taste. Spoon in the crushed ice and top up with the lemonade. Garnish with a mint sprig and serve with a stirrer and a straw.

Alternative

If liked use ginger beer and make into a short drink by halving the amount of ginger beer and pouring into a short glass over ice cubes. Add lemonade if liked.

Acapulco Gold

If you have a fresh coconut it is very easy to make your own coconut flakes. Simply break the fruit in half, reserving the coconut juice inside to add to the drink. Using a swivel vegetable peeler, simply cut off very thin flakes of the fresh coconut. These can be lightly dried out in a warm oven and this will keep the flakes for longer. Remember to store in an airtight container. Fresh flakes should be used within 2–3 days.

Ingredients   SERVES 1

4 ice cubes, crushed
3 measures pineapple juice
1 measure grapefruit juice
1 measure coconut cream
3–4 measures lemonade to top up
1 tbsp whipped cream
few coconut flakes and mint
    sprig to garnish

Method

Place the crushed ice into a cocktail shaker and pour in the pineapple and grapefruit juice. Add the coconut cream and shake for 20 seconds or until wellblended. Strain into a chilled tumbler and top up with the lemonade. Float the whipped cream on top and serve garnished with the toasted coconut flakes and mint sprig.

Alternative

Try apple juice instead of pineapple juice if preferred.

Apple of my Eye

Blackcurrants, like redcurrants, are one of the few fruits that are not available all year round. Now, when I see them in the shops or markets, I normally buy some and freeze them so that I can use them whenever I want.

Ingredients   SERVES 1

3 ice cubes

3 measures clear apple juice

1$\frac{1}{2}$ measures blackcurrant syrup

lemonade to top up

1 scoop good quality vanilla
    ice cream

wedge of red eating apple, sprig of
    blackcurrant if available and mint
    sprig to garnish

Method

Place the ice into a cocktail shaker and pour in the apple juice and blackcurrant syrup. Shake until blended then strain into a tall tumbler. Top up with the lemonade and place the scoop of ice cream on top. Garnish with the apple wedge, blackcurrant sprig if using and a mint sprig.

Alternative

Try blending 1 measure of whipped cream with the ingredients, rather than floating ice cream on top.

Bora Bora

Bora Bora is a Tahitian island that is surrounded by a lagoon and fringing reef. The centre of the island is dominated by the remnants of an extinct volcano, which has two distinct peaks. The word actually means 'peace' which is reflected in the delicious drink below.

Ingredients   SERVES 1

4 ice cubes, crushed
3 measures pineapple juice
3 measures ginger beer
1 measure coconut cream
1 measure grenadine
$\frac{1}{2}$ tsp ground ginger
1 measure freshly squeezed
    lime juice
1–2 tsp ginger syrup (use the syrup
    from a jar of stem ginger)
lime wedges to garnish

Method

Pour the pineapple juice, the ginger beer, coconut cream and grenadine together with the ground ginger to taste, the freshly squeezed lime juice and the stem ginger syrup. Shake for 20 seconds or until well blended. Place the crushed ice into a short tumbler and pour in the prepared cocktail. Garnish with the lime wedges.

Brontosaurus

The name of the drink actually means 'thunder lizard' in Greek and refers back to when dinosaurs ruled the world. This drink however is bang up to date and in the 21st century. Perfect any time, day or evening.

Ingredients   SERVES 1

4 ice cubes, crushed

3 measures red grapefruit juice

2 measures freshly squeezed
    orange juice

1 measure freshly squeezed
    lemon juice

1 measure freshly squeezed
    lime juice

$^{1}/_{2}$ measure grenadine

2–3 dashes Worcestershire sauce

orange and lemon twists plus lime
    slice to garnish

Method

Place all the fruit juices into a cocktail shaker with the grenadine and crushed ice. Shake until blended then pour into a glass and add Worcestershire sauce to taste. Serve garnished with the fruit twists.

Alternative

Replace the grapefruit with carrot juice and add a few dashes of Tabasco sauce to taste. Season with a little freshly ground black pepper and serve with a celery stick as a stirrer.

Canadian Pride

Maple syrup is the flagship where food is concerned for Canada and is used extensively in both food and drinks. It is a sweetener that is made from the sap of the maple tree. It is produced in a sugarbush, or sugarwood – these are wooded shacks where the sap is boiled down to a syrup.

Ingredients   SERVES 1

4 ice cubes
3 measures pink grapefruit juice
2 measures maple syrup
1¹/₂–2 measures freshly squeezed
   lemon juice
1 measure ginger ale
lemon rind twist to garnish

Method

Pour the grapefruit juice with the maple syrup and 1 measure of lemon juice into a cocktail shaker and shake for 30 seconds or until blended. Check for sweetness and if necessary add the remaining lemon juice and shake again. Add the ginger wine and shake briefly. Place the ice into a glass and pour over the drink. Garnish with the lemon rind twist and serve.

Alternative

Try garnishing with a slice of grapefruit rather than lemon rind.

Mickey Mouse

As with the character Mickey Mouse, this drink is loved by all the 'young at heart'. Crammed full of delicious ice cream floating on top of chilled cola, what could be better on a hot day to keep the temperature down?

Ingredients SERVES 1

3 ice cubes

5 measures chilled cola

1 scoop good quality vanilla
   ice cream

1 scoop good quality chocolate
   ice cream

1 tbsp whipped cream

$^1/_2$ tsp finely grated chocolate

Method

Place the ice cubes into a tall tumbler and pour in the chilled cola. Top with the scoops of vanilla and chocolate ice cream and sprinkle with the grated chocolate. Serve with a spoon.

Passion Cooler

It is best when using passion fruit to buy at least 4 days before you wish to use them. Allow to ripen in the fruit bowl rather than keeping in the refrigerator. It is a matter of personal preference as to whether you use the seeds.

Ingredients   SERVES 1

2 measures freshly squeezed
    orange juice
2 measures mango juice
1 measure pineapple juice
1 ripe passion fruit
$^1/_2$ ripe banana, mashed
4 ice cubes, crushed
wedges of orange, lime and
    pineapple to garnish

Method

Pour the orange, mango and pineapple juice into a cocktail shaker. Scoop out the seeds and pulp from the passion fruit and place into the cocktail shaker, together with the banana. Shake for 30 seconds or until well blended. Place the crushed ice into a tall tumbler and pour over the blended juice. Thread the fruit wedges on to a cocktail stick and place across the tumbler to garnish.

Alternative

Replace the passion fruit with 1–2 teaspoons of grenadine.

Queen Charlie

If wishing to use a fresh mango to provide the juice for this drink do make sure that the fruit is ripe and unblemished. Peel, discarding the stone then whizz in a liquidizer or food processor.

Ingredients SERVES 1

3 ice cubes
1 measure grenadine
1 measure guava juice
1 measure mango juice
lemonade to top up
maraschino cherry to garnish

Method

Pour the grenadine into a cocktail shaker together with the guava and mango juice. Add the ice and shake for 30 seconds or until blended. Pour into a short tumbler and top up with lemonade. Thread the cherry on a cocktail stick and use to garnish the glass.

Alternative

Use other tropical fruit juices according to personal preference and add a mashed banana to make a thicker drink.

Pomola

A pomelo is the largest of the citrus fruits and has a very thick green skin with thick white pith. The flesh is very fibrous and can be bitter, so be prepared to add a little more sweetness.

Ingredients   SERVES 1

3 ice cubes

2 measures pomelo juice

$^1/_2$ measure grenadine

2–3 tsp (or to taste) syrup from a jar
   of maraschino cherries

5 measures chilled cola

maraschino cherry and lime wedge
   to garnish

Method

Place the ice cubes into a tall tumbler and pour in the pomelo juice. Add the grenadine and maraschino cherry syrup and stir well. Top up with the chilled cola and serve garnished with the maraschino cherry and lime wedge.

Alternative

Replace the pomelo juice with grapefruit juice; either use yellow, pink or red grapefruit. The pink and red grapefruits are slightly sweeter than the yellow variety.

Magnificent Peach

This delicious drink is a luscious fruit salad in a glass and is perfect for hot summer days or evenings. Suitable for all ages it is very easy to vary this recipe by using different flavoured fruit juices.

Ingredients   SERVES 1

3 ice cubes
2 ripe peaches, stoned
1 measure orange juice
1–2 drops almond essence
chilled lemonade to top up
1 scoop raspberry sorbet
peach and fresh raspberries
   to garnish

Method

Slice the peaches and place in a blender or smoothie machine with the orange juice and almond essence. Blend until smooth then strain into a glass. Add the ice then pour in the chilled lemonade and top up with a scoop of raspberry sorbet. Place a long-handled spoon into the glass and serve.

Alternative

The peach can be replaced with nectarines, either the white or yellow fleshed varieties. Use according to personal preference or availability, but do make sure they are ripe.

Tarzan's Juicy Cooler

This drink might not mean that you will be swinging through the trees after drinking it but it will certainly keep you cool when the weather gets hot.

Ingredients   SERVES 1

3 ice cubes

3 measures freshly squeezed
   orange juice

3 measures pineapple juice

$^1/_2$ measure lemon juice

50 g/2 oz ripe strawberries,
   lightly rinsed

chilled sparkling water to top up

1 scoop strawberry ice cream

mint sprig to garnish

Method

Place all the fruit juices into a blender or liquidizer. Reserve one of the strawberries for garnish. Slice the remaining strawberries and place into the blender or liquidizer and whizz for 30 seconds. Strain then pour into a tall tumbler and add the ice cubes. Top up with the chilled sparkling water and float the strawberry ice cream on top. Garnish with the strawberry and mint sprig.

Summer Rain

When using raspberries in a purée it is always a good idea to sieve the purée afterwards to remove the pips which, if still present, can seriously affect the feel of the drink.

Ingredients   SERVES 1

4 ice cubes

1 measure freshly squeezed
   orange juice

1 measure freshly squeezed
   lemon juice

2 measures mango juice

50 g/2 oz fresh ripe raspberries,
   lightly rinsed

chilled lemonade to top up

1 scoop lemon sorbet (or water ice)

Method

Pour the fruit juices into a blender. Reserve 2–3 raspberries for garnish and add the remainder to the blender. Whizz for 30 seconds or until well blended and then strain. Place the ice cubes into a tall tumbler and pour over the strained drink. Top up with the lemonade and float the lemon sorbet on top. Garnish with the reserved raspberries and serve.

Alternative

Ice cream can replace the sorbet if liked; try a scoop or two of chocolate ice cream and then sprinkle with a little grated chocolate – delicious or what?

Fruit Flip

It is always best when possible to use organic produce, as they are grown without the aid of artificial fertilizers or pesticides. They can be used with confidence and are guaranteed to be chemical free.

Ingredients   SERVES 1

3 ice cubes
1 medium sized orange,
    preferably organic
1 ripe lemon, preferably organic
1 medium organic egg
1–2 tsp (or to taste) caster sugar
orange and lemon twists to garnish

Method

Squeeze out the juice from both the orange and lemon. Whisk the egg with sugar to taste until creamy then gradually whisk in the orange and lemon juice. Strain into a short tumbler and top up with ice cubes. Garnish with the orange and lemon twists and serve.

Pine Lime Sparkle

It is recommended that in order to maintain a healthy lifestyle we should all eat at least five portions of fruit or vegetables a day. Fruit juice counts for the same as a piece of fruit. Here you have the recommended daily dose in one glass.

Ingredients   SERVES 1

3 ice cubes
3 measures pineapple juice
1 measure freshly squeezed
    lime juice
2 measures freshly squeezed
    lemon juice
1–2 tsp (or to taste) icing sugar
chilled lemonade to top up
1 small wedge pineapple, lemon and
    lime twists to garnish

Method

Place the pineapple juice with the lime and lemon juice into a cocktail shaker and add 1 teaspoon of icing sugar. Shake for 30 seconds or until blended. Taste for sweetness and if necessary add the remaining icing sugar and shake again. Place the ice into a tall tumbler and pour in the blended juice. Top up with the lemonade and garnish with the pineapple wedge and lemon and lime twists.

Alternative

For a sweeter drink replace either the lime or lemon juice with orange juice.

Summertime Cooler

If you have a smoothie machine, it can be used for all the fruit-based drinks. It will blend the fruits to a good consistency and ensure that all the valuable fibre is included in the drink.

Ingredients   SERVES 1

3 ice cubes, crushed

50 g/2 oz ripe strawberries,
   lightly rinsed

50 g/2 oz raspberries, lightly rinsed

1 ripe plum, rinsed, stoned and sliced

1 tsp clear honey

5 measures chilled sparkling water

1 scoop good quality ice cream

mint sprig to garnish

Method

Place the fruits into a blender together with the honey and whizz for 30 seconds. Rub through a sieve and pour into a tumbler. Add the ice cubes and top up with the chilled sparkling water. Place the scoop of ice cream on top and add a long-handled spoon to the glass. Serve garnished with a mint sprig.

Alternative

Replace the sparkling water with ginger beer, lemonade or soda water. Use lemonade if a sweet drink is required.

Prohibition Punch

Prohibition occurred in many countries in the early twentieth century. Most people associate Prohibition with the United States, where it was illegal to sell, make, transport or consume alcohol between 1920–33. Russia, Iceland, Norway and Finland also enforced prohibition laws around this period. This Punch would have been ideal to serve then.

Ingredients SERVES 10

1 red apple, rinsed
4–5 mint sprigs
8–10 ice cubes
3 measures sugar syrup (see page 10)
600 ml/1 pt clear apple juice
300 ml/$^1/_2$ pt cranberry juice
300 ml/$^1/_2$ pt cold freshly brewed
   peppermint tea

Method

Core the apple and chop, then place into a large glass jug together with the mint sprigs and ice cubes. Pour in the sugar syrup together with the apple and cranberry juice. Stir in the cold tea, stir well and allow it to stand for at least 20 minutes to allow the flavours to mingle. Serve in short tumblers, ensuring that each glass gets 1–2 pieces of apple.

Spicy Cooler

The addition of spices to this Punch infuse it with such incredible flavour that the alcohol is not missed at all. Try serving it to your friends and listen to all the praise they will heap on you.

Ingredients
SERVES 10

600 ml/1 pt orange juice

1 lemon, preferably organic

300 ml/½ pt pineapple juice

300 ml/½ pt freshly brewed tea

3–4 tbsp (or to taste) clear honey

small piece root ginger, peeled and grated

6 whole cloves

2 cinnamon sticks, lightly bruised

1 small orange and lemon, preferably organic

Method

Pour the orange juice into a heavy–based saucepan. Thinly pare the rind from the lemon and squeeze out the juice. Add to the saucepan together with the pineapple juice and the freshly brewed tea. Add the honey together with the grated root ginger, the whole cloves and cinnamon sticks. Heat gently until hot but take care not to allow the liquid to boil. Thinly slice the orange and cut into small wedges. Add to the saucepan and heat for a further 10 minutes. Strain into a heatproof bowl. Serve either warm or cool, ensuring that each glass gets a wedge or two of orange.

Aromatic Cup

The fragrant aroma of this Cup is due to the addition of the star anise, cinnamon sticks, cardamom pods and passion fruit.

Ingredients   SERVES 10

10 ice cubes
600 ml/1 pt clear apple juice
300 ml/^{1}/$_2$ pt freshly brewed
   green tea
2 ripe limes, preferably organic
6 cardamom pods, lightly cracked
3 whole star anise
2 cinnamon sticks, lightly bruised
^{1}/$_2$–1 small red chilli, deseeded
2 ripe passion fruit
300 ml/^{1}/$_2$ pt chilled sparkling water
100 g/4 oz lychees, stoned
   and chopped
cinnamon sticks to serve (optional)

Method

Pour the apple juice and tea into a heavy–based saucepan. Finely peel the rind from one of the limes and squeeze out the juice from both. Add to the saucepan together with all the spices including the chilli. Bring slowly to the boil then remove from the heat. Scoop out the pulp and seeds from the passion fruit and add to the saucepan. Cover and leave for at least 1 hour. Strain into a punchbowl; add the ice cubes then stir in the sparkling water and the lychees. Serve in short tumblers with a cinnamon stick to use as a stirrer.

Barbary Ale

Ingredients
SERVES 10

10 ice cubes
4 large oranges, preferably organic
2 ripe lemons, preferably organic
600 ml/1 pt filtered or mineral water
100 g/4 oz light muscovado sugar
2 tsp ground cinnamon
1½ tsp ground mixed spice
600 ml/1 pt ginger beer
1 lemon for garnish

Method
Thinly peel the rind from one of the oranges and squeeze the juice from all the fruit. Place the rind and juices into a heavy–based saucepan. Add the water and sugar. Spoon the cinnamon and spice into a small bowl and blend to a smooth paste with 2 tablespoons of water. Stir into the saucepan. Stir frequently over a gentle heat until the sugar has completely dissolved. Continue to heat gently for 15–20 minutes, stirring occasionally until hot. Remove from the heat and allow to cool for at least 1 hour before straining into a punchbowl. Stir in the ginger beer. Thinly slice the lemon and cut each slice into triangles. Add to the punchbowl with the ice cubes. Serve cold in short tumblers.

Muscovado sugar is unrefined sugar with a strong molasses or treacle flavour. It is very dark in colour and slightly sticky.

Index